ANNUAL 2005!

MATCH Editor > Simon Caney **Art Director** > Darryl Tooth **Annual Editor** > Ian Foster **Assistant Editor** > Kevin Hughes **Production Editor** > James Bandy **Deputy Production Editor** > Kevin Pettman **Senior Writer** > Giles Milton **Sub-Editor/Writers** > Mark Bailey, Darren Cross, Matt Read **Senior Designer** > Martin Barry **Designer** Calum Booth **Staff Photographer** > Phil Bagnall **Cartoonist** > Russ Carvell **And the rest of the MATCH team** > Dawn Brown, Isobel Cardew & Susan Good

THE UK'S BEST-SELLING WEEKLY FOOTBALL MAGAZINE!

Bushfield House, Orton Centre, Peterborough, PE2 5UW ✆ Tel: 01733 237111 Fax: 01733 288150 ✉ e-mail: match.magazine@emap.com

D1180284

PLANET FOOTY!

DID YOU KNOW...?

RONALDO'S SON IS CALLED RONALD! THE REAL MADRID AND BRAZIL STAR MUST HAVE THOUGHT FOR AGES TO COME UP WITH THAT NAME!

NICE ONE, DAD!

Wanna know my favourite movie? Check out page 38 to find out!

HEY THIERRY, I CAN ALSO TIE MY OWN LACES!

HEY GIRLS, TAKE A LOOK AT THESE LOVELY LEGS!

WELL DONE RONALDO, WELL DONE!

PULL YER SOCKS UP!

RONALDO'S TRIBUTE TO HENRY!

IS RON WEARING TIGHTS?

CRISTIANO RONALDO PULLS HIS SOCKS ABOVE HIS KNEES AS A TRIBUTE TO HIS FAVOURITE FOOTY PLAYER – THIERRY HENRY! ALTHOUGH HENRY AND RONALDO ARE BIG PREMIERSHIP RIVALS, RON IS STILL A MASSIVE FAN OF THE FLYING FRENCH STRIKER! IT'S WELL TRENDY TO WEAR KNEE-HIGH SOCKS ON THE FOOTY PITCH RIGHT NOW – BUT NOBODY LOOKS AS GOOD AS TEZZA HENRY!

TRANSFER RECORDS! TOP WORLD TRANSFER: ZINEDINE ZIDANE, JUVENTUS TO REAL MADRID

FIVE GREATEST ENGLAND WINS!

1 England 4-2 West Germany
World Cup final, 1966

2 Germany 1-5 England
World Cup qualifier, 2001

3 England 1-0 Argentina
World Cup 2002

4 England 4-1 Holland
Euro '96

5 England 2-0 Turkey
Euro 2004 qualifier, 2003

THESE GUYS LOVE IT TOO!

I'M NUMBER ONE WHEN IT COMES TO WEARING SOCKS!

MATEJA KEZMAN!

DAVID BENTLEY!

LOOK AT THESE BAD BOYS!

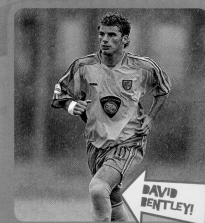

JUAN PABLO ANGEL!

CAMPING... WITH IVAN CAMPO!

I LOVE CAMPING, ME!

ROOAARRR!

OOH ECK!

THIS WEEK, CAMPO GOES CAMPING IN... LONDON ZOO!

GERRARD'S NEW INSPIRATION!

Steven Gerrard has found some new inspiration for footy – his baby daughter Lily! All together now – ahh!

My Favourite... HOLIDAY SPOT!

by Gary Neville, Man. United

"My favourite holiday spot is Malta! I've got an apartment there and I love it. My brother Phil, and a few current and ex-Man. United team-mates – like David Beckham – have been out there!"

STOP PRESS... STOP PRESS... STOP PRESS...
The truth is out – Ruud van Nistelrooy isn't very good!
Who says? Him! "I realise that if I don't work very hard
then I can't be very good," the Man. United star revealed.
"I'm not an exceptional player and that's why I have to
play every game like it's my last!" That's harsh, Ruud!

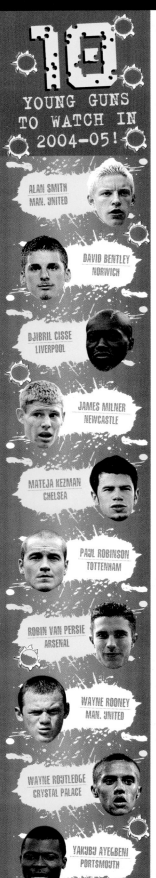

10
YOUNG GUNS TO WATCH IN 2004-05!

ALAN SMITH
MAN. UNITED

DAVID BENTLEY
NORWICH

DJIBRIL CISSE
LIVERPOOL

JAMES MILNER
NEWCASTLE

MATEJA KEZMAN
CHELSEA

PAUL ROBINSON
TOTTENHAM

ROBIN VAN PERSIE
ARSENAL

WAYNE ROONEY
MAN. UNITED

WAYNE ROUTLEDGE
CRYSTAL PALACE

YAKUBU AYEGBENI
PORTSMOUTH

BRAZIL TRAINING!

I'M KAKA! WHAT A COOL NAME, EH?

FIRST ONE TO DROP THE BALL GETS NO DINNER!

The Brazil lads get legless!

HANDBALL REF!

PHEW! TIME FOR TEA NOW! YUM, YUM!

I'LL RACE YOU OVER THERE, RONALDO!

The stars get their orders from the coach!

TOP 5 OLDEST PREMIERSHIP PLAYERS!

KEVIN POOLE
BOLTON ★ 41

NIGEL MARTYN
EVERTON ★ 38

COLIN COOPER
MIDDLESBROUGH ★ 37

LES FERDINAND
BOLTON ★ 37

FERNANDO HIERRO
BOLTON ★ 36

MATCH FULFILLED A DREAM WHEN WE TRAINED WITH THE BRAZIL TEAM! BETTER STILL, WE TOOK A CAMERA SO WE COULD SHOW YOU ALL THE BEHIND-THE-SCENES ACTION AND PRANKS. CHECK IT OUT!

MATCH went dizzy watching their skills!

...but even Brazil legends can fall on their asses!

Gilberto was one of the stars on show...

BROOKLYN LOVES FOOTY!

MATCH reckons Brooklyn Beckham is his dad's biggest fan! Everywhere Becks goes, Brooklyn's watching his dad play footy. Don't believe us? Check out our snaps!

My Favourite...
MUSIC!

By Petr Cech, Chelsea
"I'm a big fan of U2 and the Red Hot Chili Peppers. I suppose I'm a bit of a rocker, really!"

SCORER: MARK HUGHES, 38 YEARS & 150 DAYS... MOST PREMIERSHIP TITLES: MAN. UNITED, EIGHT...

MATCH! ANNUAL 2005 > 7

DID YOU KNOW...?

ARSENE WENGER MAY LOOK LIKE A KNOW-IT-ALL PROFESSOR – BUT THAT'S BECAUSE HE'S GOT A DEGREE IN ECONOMICS FROM THE UNIVERSITY OF STRASBOURG!

KRAZY QUOTE

"He's a killer. He's the king of the box, and with me beside him, maybe he'll score even more than he has!"

Newcastle's Patrick Kluivert reveals Alan Shearer really is a 'deadly' striker!

VAN PERSIE'S NIGHTMARE MEMORIES!

WHEN ARSENAL STAR ROBIN VAN PERSIE was a youngster, he was attacked on the pitch by a bunch of crazy opposition fans! The Holland forward was in the middle of playing for Feyenoord in a reserve game when rival fans got on to the pitch.

They attacked Van Persie, who only escaped when a brave member of the rival coaching staff jumped on top of the Dutch ace to protect him! "I thought I was going to die," says Van Persie. "It was the most horrific experience of my life and it left me feeling totally traumatised."

Van Persie had a few sleepless nights, but the £3 million star is now set on ripping up Premiership defences for new club Arsenal!

WHAT'S GOING ON IN THE MIND OF...

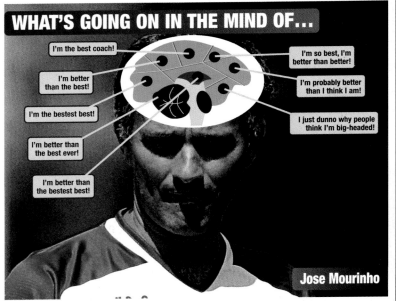

I'm the best coach!

I'm so best, I'm better than better!

I'm better than the best!

I'm probably better than I think I am!

I'm the bestest best!

I just dunno why people think I'm big-headed!

I'm better than the best ever!

I'm better than the bestest best!

Jose Mourinho

HOW TO BE A GAL

RULE 1 Argue over who's going to take the free-kicks!

STAND BACK, FIGO. I RECKON I CAN SCORE THIS FREE-KICK!

ER, BECKS, THIS IS JUST THE KICK-OFF!

RULE 4 Sell five million shirts in the Far East!

RULE 5 Stuff Man. United or another massive club!

FA CUP RECORDS! MOST GOALS IN CUP FINALS: IAN RUSH, FIVE... MOST CUP FINAL WINS: MAN. UNITED, 11...

8 < *MATCH!* ANNUAL 2005

WHAT BOOTS DOES...
ARJEN ROBBEN WEAR?

Adidas F-50s!

6.7 MILLION!
That's how much Patrick Kluivert was paid each year by Barcelona. It made him the world's best-paid footballer!

I'M ROLLING IN IT, FOR SURE!

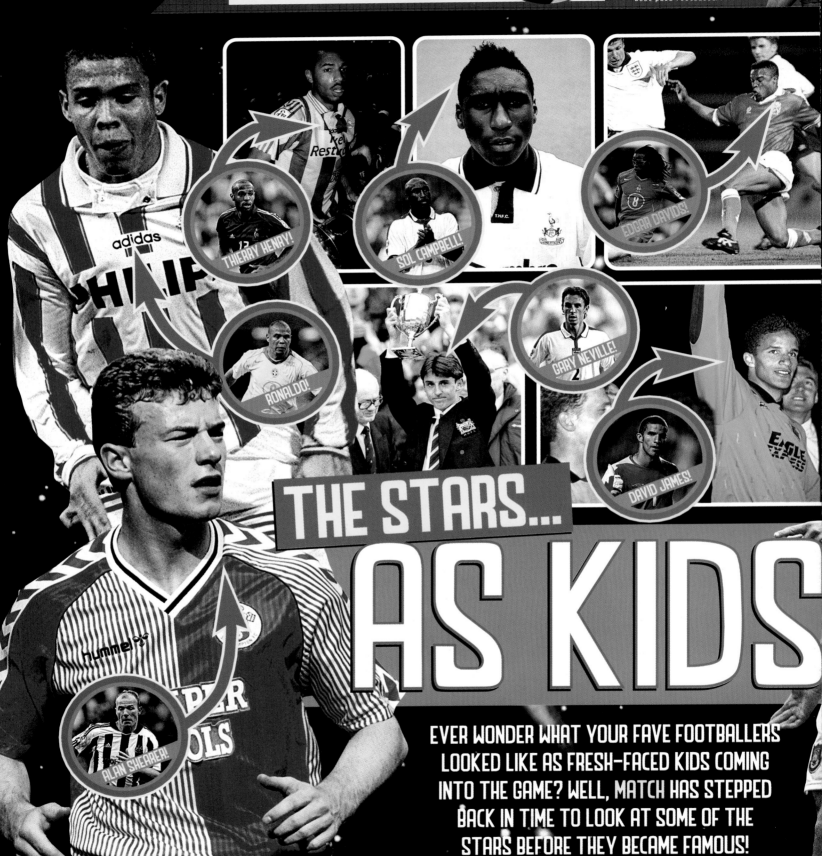

THIERRY HENRY!

SOL CAMPBELL!

EDGAR DAVIDS!

RONALDO!

GARY NEVILLE!

DAVID JAMES!

ALAN SHEARER!

THE STARS...
AS KIDS

EVER WONDER WHAT YOUR FAVE FOOTBALLERS LOOKED LIKE AS FRESH-FACED KIDS COMING INTO THE GAME? WELL, MATCH HAS STEPPED BACK IN TIME TO LOOK AT SOME OF THE STARS BEFORE THEY BECAME FAMOUS!

EUROPEAN CUP RECORDS! MOST FINAL DEFEATS: BENFICA & JUVENTUS, 5; MOST CUP WINS: REA

USA STARS OF THE FUTURE!

FREDDY ADU — DC UNITED
LANDON DONOVAN — SAN JOSE EARTHQUAKES
JONNY SPECTOR — MAN. UNITED
"I'M JONNY SPECTOR, SUPER HERO!"
DAMARCUS BEASLEY — CHICAGO FIRE
"HEY, MASCARENHAS!"
BRIAN MASCARENHAS — ATLANTA

RIO FERDINAND!

FRANK LAMPARD!

YOUNG GUNS!

SIX UP-AND-COMING STRIKERS!

ALBERTO GILARDINO
Parma
They say he's the new Paolo Rossi – an Italian striking legend who won the 1982 World Cup!

JAVIER CHEVANTON
Monaco
The Uruguay youngster is in red-hot form – and should be a hit with new club Monaco!

MARCELO ZALAYETA
Juventus
After waiting his turn at Juve, the young Uruguayan striker is ready to rock Serie A!

LUKAS PODOLSKI
FC Koln
The German Wayne Rooney should be a big hit in Germany after appearing at Euro 2004!

PEGGUY LUYINDULA
Lyon
The French ace is hot property and has been eyed up by AC Milan and Monaco!

ADRIANO
Inter Milan
After starring at the Copa America, Brazilian star Adriano is tipped for big things!

How to celebrate like... FRANK LAMPARD!

FLY LIKE A LITTLE BIRDY!

BECKS BITES BACK!

GRRRR!

Watch out everyone – David Beckham is gonna stuff your criticism down your throats! Becks has got really fed up with everyone dissing him for his Real Madrid and England displays this year – and he's bitten back! "People have criticised me, and to send those remarks back where they came from is a goal for me," says a determined Becks. "I want to do well in the competitions we're competing for and perform well!" You tell 'em Dave!

My Favourite... TV SHOWS!

by Shaka Hislop, Portsmouth

"I watch 'Seinfeld' and that's about it. I've got four young daughters so I've not got much control over the TV set! My two-year-old is into things like 'Barney' and 'Teletubbies' right now though!"

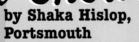

TOP FIVE BLOND BOMBSHELLS!

Djibril Cisse LIVERPOOL

Eidur Gudjohnsen CHELSEA

Antti Niemi SOUTHAMPTON

Guti REAL MADRID

Lee Trundle WREXHAM

THE STORY SO FAR!

WE ARE ZE ARSENAL, YOU WON'T SCORE AGAINST US!

It was against Arsenal in October 2002 that Rooney made his name.

GERRIN'!

The Gunners hadn't counted on 16-year-old Roonaldo...

YEAAAHHH, I'M A RECORD BREAKER!

YEAAHH!

...becoming the youngest Premiership goalscorer ever...

WOOHOO!

ER, WAYNE... CAN YOU GET DOWN NOW – YER GETTIN' HEAVY, MATE!

...and ruining their unbeaten run!

It didn't matter though...

EAT THIS, KOALA HEAD!

...coz Rooney soon won his first England cap against the Aussies!

I'LL STUFF YOU TURKEY BOYS!

Soon after he starred in the vital Euro 2004 qualifier against Turkey...

WHO'S DA NUTS?!

...before nabbing his first ever England goal against Macedonia.

Then he hit four goals and was a massive star!

BETTER LUCK NEXT TIME, SON!

Rooney did well against France but still ended up losing!

GOAL, GOAL, GOAL, GOAL! DAT MAKES FOUR, I RECKON!

Sadly, a broken metatarsal wrecked his tournament...

OUCH!

...but what a career so far!

YOU'VE SEEN NOTHING YET, MATCH READERS! BRING IT ON!

MIDFIELD M

ZINEDINE
ZIDANE
PAGE 16

RONALDINHO
PAGE 22

JAY-JAY
OKOCHA
PAGE 42

EGASTARS!

MATCH *checks out the amazing careers of five Midfield Megastars!*

When you're talking about the most skilful players in world football, they don't come much better than Zinedine Zidane, Ronaldinho, Jay-Jay Okocha, Luis Figo and Pavel Nedved.

These midfield megastars are blessed with the most outrageous skill you'll ever see on a football pitch. They can control a cross-field ball with a single touch, they can beat players with a flash trick that makes a defender look silly – and they can go on a magical dribble as they weave past their opponents towards goal.

Our five megastars have dazzled fans at the best clubs in the world, and for the most successful countries in the world – and together they've won every major trophy in world football! But how did they become such talented players?

MATCH looks back at their sensational careers to find out how it all began, starting with a shy young Frenchman at Cannes called Zinedine Zidane. Check it out!

LUIS FIGO

PAGE 52

PAVEL NEDVED

PAGE 74

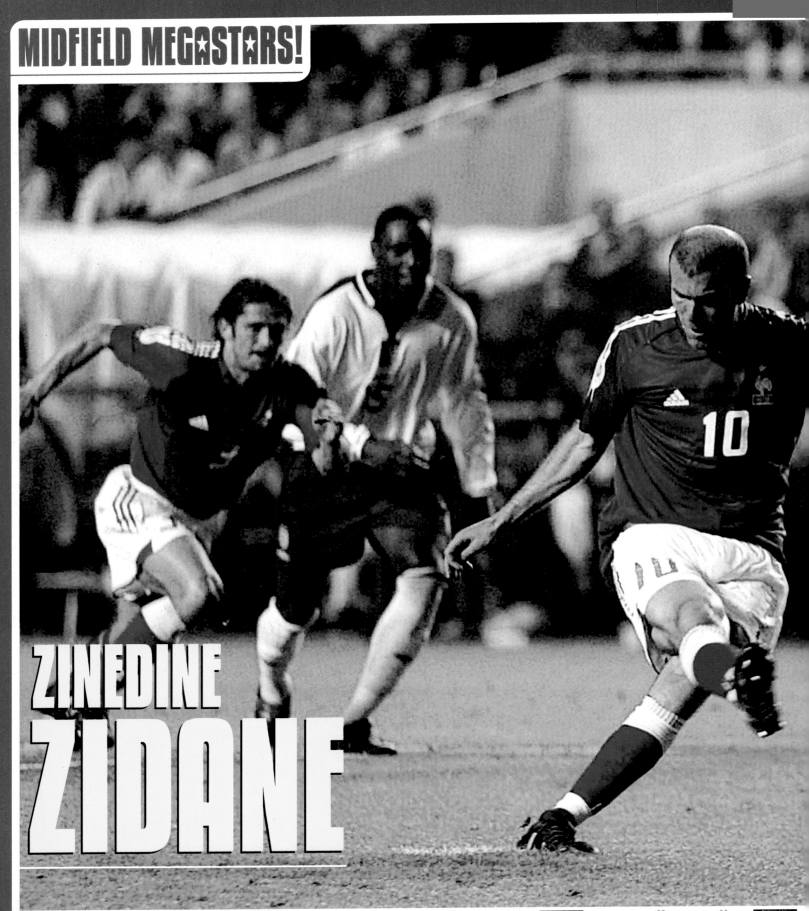

MIDFIELD MEGASTARS!

ZINEDINE ZIDANE

Zidane Timeline...

June
LITTLE ZIZOU!
Zidane is born in Marseille to Algerian parents.
1972

August
CANNES CAN!
Signs for his first professional club, French side Cannes.
1988

June
BORD-OH!
Leaves Cannes to join French rivals Bordeaux.

August
DOUBLE DEBUT!
Makes full French debut and scores twice against the Czech Republic after coming on as a substitute.
1992

1994

May
UEFA BLOW!
Helps Bordeaux to the UEFA Cup final, but they lose to Bayern Munich.

June
SEMI SLUMP!
Takes France to the semi-finals of Euro '96 but they lose to the Czech Republic.
1996

July
JUVE JOY!
Moves from Bordeaux to Italian giants Juventus.
1997

May
TROPHY HAUL!
Finishes first Juventus season with three trophies.

May
JUVE LOSER!
Loses again in the European Cup final as Juve are beaten 1-0 by Real Madrid.
1998

July
VIVE LE FRANCE!
Scores twice as France beat Brazil 3-0 to win the World Cup for the first time.

"Everyone loves Zizou. He is the star of the French team. He is part of the generation that has won everything."
Patrick Vieira

MATCH reveals the brilliant career of *ZINEDINE ZIDANE!*

There's no doubt that when it comes to skilful midfielders in the history of the game, there have been very few on the same level as French magician Zinedine Zidane!

Zidane's a master of control and possession. He rarely gives the ball away and can keep hold of it even with opponents snapping away at his heels. But there's also an end product with Zidane and he delivers the goods. His trophy haul is impressive – 'Zizou' has won league titles in Italy with Juventus and in Spain with Real Madrid, and he's also won the Champions League, scoring the winning goal in 2002 with a brilliant volley!

And then there's his success with France. In 1998, Zidane scored twice in the final to win the World Cup, and two years later led his country to the Euro 2000 title.

On top of that, the midfielder has been named FIFA World Player Of The Year three times and is the most expensive footballer of all time, having been bought by Real Madrid for £46.5 million! He's a true midfield megastar, so MATCH takes a closer look at the fantastic Frenchman's amazing career!

CAREER FACTFILE!

Born: June 23, 1972 in Marseille

Nationality: French

Position: Midfielder

Height: 6ft 2ins

Weight: 12st 6lbs

Former clubs: Cannes, Bordeaux, Juventus

Signed: From Juventus for £46.5 million on July 9, 2001

Real Madrid debut: v Real Zaragoza, August 19, 2001

Real Madrid games/goals: 127 games, 31 goals (August 2001 to May 2004)

France caps/goals: 93 games, 26 goals (August 1994 to June 2004)

WORLD'S NO.1!
Voted FIFA World Player Of The Year. Zidane later wins the award again in 2000 and 2003.

February

1999

EURO CHAMPS!
Wins the European Championships with France after a 'Golden Goal' victory over Italy.

July

2000

October

BUTT BAN!
Sent off for headbutting Hamburg's Jochen Kientz in the Champions League. Banned for five games.

REAL DEAL!
Leaves Juve and signs for Real Madrid in world record £46.5 million deal.

July

2001

VOLLEY GOOD!
Scores a stunning volley as Real beat Bayer Leverkusen 2-1 in the Champions League final.

May

2002

August

SUPER SHOW!
Wins the European Super Cup, beating Feyenoord 3-1, and lifts the World Club Cup four months later.

June

TITLE TIME!
Wins La Liga with Real Madrid.

2003

June

FRANCE FAIL!
Skippers France at Euro 2004, but the holders crash out to Greece in the quarter-finals.

2004

1996

BORDEAUX CUP RUN!

Zinedine Zidane shot to fame outside his native France thanks to Bordeaux's amazing run to the UEFA Cup final in 1996. The club played in the previous summer's InterToto Cup to qualify for the competition proper in 1995-96 – and just kept on winning! They beat German side Karlsruhe in the preliminary round and then saw off the challenge of Vardar Skopje, Rotor Volgograd, Real Betis, mighty Italian side AC Milan and Slavia Prague to meet Bundesliga super club Bayern Munich in the two-legged final. Unfortunately, that was where their UEFA Cup fairytale ended. Bordeaux were outclassed 5-1 on aggregate, but Zidane's name had now been fully established around Europe. What would happen to him next?

1996

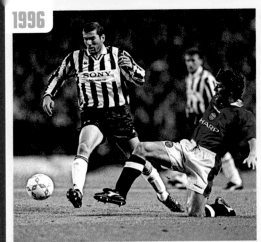

JUVENTUS JOY!

After playing for France at Euro '96, Zidane prepared for a new challenge. Bordeaux sold him to one of Europe's biggest clubs – Juventus! The Italian aces had just won the Champions League so Zidane had plenty to live up to, but his first season in Turin was an amazing success. In November, Juve beat River Plate to lift the World Club Championship, and a few months later they demolished PSG 9-2 on aggregate to win the European Super Cup. Juventus also won Serie A at the end of the 1996-97 season, making it three trophies for Zidane in his first campaign in Italy!

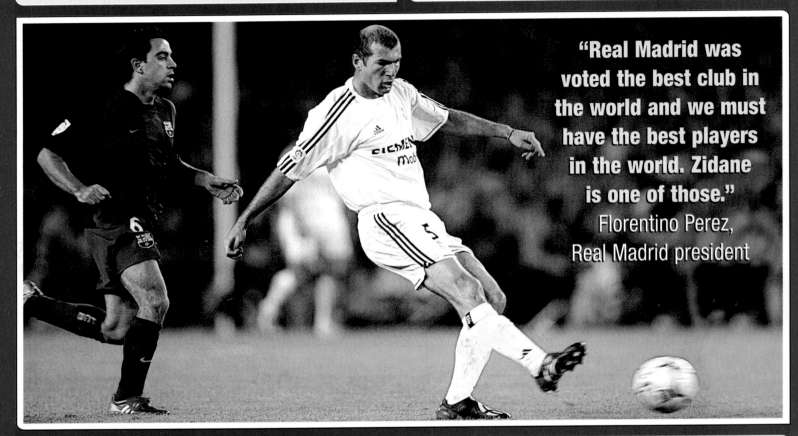

"Real Madrid was voted the best club in the world and we must have the best players in the world. Zidane is one of those."
Florentino Perez, Real Madrid president

1997

EUROPEAN CUP CURSE!

Zidane's Juventus team continued to dominate in Italy, winning Serie A again in 1997-98 ahead of Inter Milan. It was a different story in the Champions League, though – Juventus had a side packed with stars when they reached the 1997 final against unfancied German outfit Borussia Dortmund, but Dortmund produced a huge shock. Juve went 2-0 down after half an hour, and although Alessandro Del Piero pulled one back, Dortmund added a third shortly afterwards to seal a 3-1 win. But just a year later, Juve and Zidane reached the Champions League final again. Their 1998 opponents were Real Madrid, the venue was Amsterdam, but the outcome was the same. Zidane was denied again, with Real winning 1-0 thanks to Predrag Mijatovic's goal. Would Zizou's European Cup luck ever change?

1998

CHAMPION OF THE WORLD!

As the hosts of the 1998 World Cup, France had high hopes of winning the competition for the first time. Zidane was their key player, but he didn't make the best of starts! In France's second game – a 4-0 victory against Saudi Arabia – Zizou was red-carded for stamping on an opponent! He was suspended for the next two matches, returning for a tough quarter-final against Italy. France won that on penalties – with Zidane scoring his kick – and came from behind to beat Croatia in the semi-final. The final was against the holders Brazil, and Zidane rose to the challenge. He scored two first-half headers as France coasted to a 3-0 win, and the biggest prize in football belonged to Les Bleus at last!

1998

WORLD'S BEST!

Great players win the World Player Of The Year award. Fantastic players win it twice. Zinedine Zidane has won it three times! Zizou first claimed the award in 1998 after leading France to the World Cup – then won it again in 2000 and a third time in 2003, beating fellow countryman Thierry Henry. The only other player to ever win the FIFA prize three times is Brazil's Ronaldo. "It doesn't matter how many times you win an award, it's always very special and it is even more special when it is voted by the coaches," said Zidane. "It is a major honour for me and I am very proud to have won it."

2000

EURO BOY!

Zidane again showed his ability to win games at the very highest level at the 2000 European Championships. France lost to Holland in the group stages, but they still qualified for the knockout phase, which is when Zizou really began to turn it on. His classy free-kick set France on the way to a 2-1 quarter-final victory over Spain, and he showed ice-cool nerves to score a penalty in the closing seconds of extra-time to beat Portugal in the semi-finals. The Euro 2000 final was a close call. Trailing Italy going into the last minute of normal time, France were rescued by Sylvain Wiltord's 90th-minute equaliser, and when David Trezeguet struck a Golden Goal winner, Zidane had captured his second major international honour in two years!

2001

TRANSFER RECORD!

Following Zidane's international achievements he became a target for other big clubs. They don't get much bigger than Juventus, but even the Italians were powerless to fight off Real Madrid's interest. And when the Spanish kings broke the world transfer record, paying £46.5 million, Zizou made the big move to La Liga! "It is an honour to come to Real Madrid," explained Zidane. "I have been awaiting this moment. I have spent five years at Juve and now was the time to come to Spain. I am very happy to sign for the best club in the world." Real president Florentino Perez added: "Real Madrid was voted the best club in the world by FIFA and we must have the best players in the world. Zidane is one of those."

2002

EURO CHAMP!

If Zidane moved to Real Madrid to nail his Champions League jinx, he didn't have to wait long! He'd lost the European Cup final twice with Juve, but he won it in his first season at Real – scoring the winner in the 2002 victory over Bayer Leverkusen. The goal will go down as one of the best in Zidane's career. After Raul's opener had been cancelled out by Leverkusen's Lucio, Real's Roberto Carlos floated a cross over. The ball hung in the air on the edge of the penalty area and when it dropped, Zidane struck a beautiful left-foot volley which nearly ripped the net. It won the match for Real and Zidane finally got his hands on the European Cup, making up for his previous disappointments in the finals.

2002

WORLD CUP WOE!

With Zidane in superb form after his first season at Real, big things were expected of France at the 2002 World Cup in South Korea & Japan. The holders were favourites to win the tournament again, but before it even started things went badly wrong for Zizou when he injured his left thigh. The problem ruled him out of France's opening two matches, so all he could do was watch as Senegal pulled off a surprise win, and Uruguay frustrated Les Bleus – holding them to a 0-0 draw. With his thigh heavily strapped, Zidane returned for the must-win match with Denmark, but even he was unable to inspire his country to victory. France needed to win 2-0 to go through to the next round, but it was Denmark who won 2-0 to leave Zidane and the holders down and out. "It was our worst nightmare to go out at this stage," Zidane admitted afterwards. "But that's football."

2004

ZZ'S DEADLY DOUBLE!

After Real Madrid's late-season slip in form saw them blow the league title, Spanish Cup final and Champions League, Euro 2004 was Zidane's last chance of glory that year. France's surprising quarter-final defeat to Greece put an end to those hopes, but Zidane still delivered two of the finest moments of the tournament to remind the watching world of his class. In France's opening match against England, Les Bleus trailed 1-0 going into the final minute, when they won a free-kick on the edge of the penalty area. England formed a wall, but Zidane stepped up to calmly curl the ball around it and into the net for the equaliser! Just seconds later, Thierry Henry won a penalty and Zizou – after pausing to be sick on the pitch – stroked his spot-kick past David James to make it 2-1. In the space of two minutes, the midfield megastar had produced flashes of his undoubted genius and France had won from nowhere. Pure class!

DID YOU KNOW...?

A SNAIL NAMED AFTER SPEEDY ENGLAND STRIKER MICHAEL OWEN HAS BEEN DECLARED THE FASTEST IN THE WORLD! OWEN, WHO IS OWNED BY EIGHT-YEAR-OLD JOE CLARKE, WON THE WORLD CHAMPIONSHIP SNAIL RACE AFTER SQUELCHING 13 INCHES IN JUST OVER 2 MINUTES!

I'm the fastest thing on one slimy leg!

Kaka wears the No.22 shirt for Milan because it's the same as his birthday – April 22, 1982!

Milan bought him from Sao Paulo in 2000. He signed a five-year deal said to be worth £5.5 million!

He is known in Brazil as 'O Fenomeno', which translates as 'The Phenomenon'!

Kaka almost didn't make it as a footballer, after a swimming pool accident left him with bad injuries. Luckily, he made a full recovery!

His first goal for Milan was against fierce rivals Inter, and he went on to bag ten for the season!

His younger brother came up with the nickname Kaka, and he's used it ever since!

He was born in Brasilia but grew up in Sao Paulo – the first top footy team the midfielder played for!

Although he's only recently shot to fame, Kaka was a part of Brazil's 2002 World Cup-winning squad, and he made one brief appearance as a substitute!

Kaka's full name is Ricardo Izecson Dos Santos Leite. Phew!

Kaka is a big computer game fan and always used to choose AC Milan whenever he played a footy game on his PlayStation!

10 THINGS YOU DIDN'T KNOW ABOUT...
KAKA!

AC MILAN and **BRAZIL** wonderkid **KAKA** is one of the hottest properties in footy, but how much do you know about him? Get the knowledge here!

WORLD SUPER STRIKERS

WSS

DIDIER DROGBA · CHELSEA

MIDFIELD MEGASTARS!

RONALDINHO

Ronaldinho Timeline...

March

RONNY'S HERE!
Ronaldinho de Assis Moreira born in Porto Alegre, Brazil.

1980

October

PRO TIME!
Signs first professional contract with local club Gremio.

September

WORLD JOY!
Helps Brazil to win the World Under-17 Championship in Egypt.

1997

June

DEBUT DAY!
Wins his first senior cap for Brazil against Latvia, after hitting 15 goals in 14 games for Gremio.

July

COPA KING!
Makes Brazil's Copa America squad and scores a stunning goal against Venezuela as Brazil win the trophy.

August

HAT-TRICK HERO!
Scores three goals against Saudi Arabia in the Confederations Cup semi-finals.

1999

April

PSG PAIN!
Leaves Gremio for Paris St Germain, but his debut is delayed over a contract dispute.

August

PLAY ME!
Makes PSG debut at last after FIFA step in on the transfer row.

2001

November

'GERS GRIEF!
PSG crash out of the UEFA Cup to Glasgow Rangers on penalties.

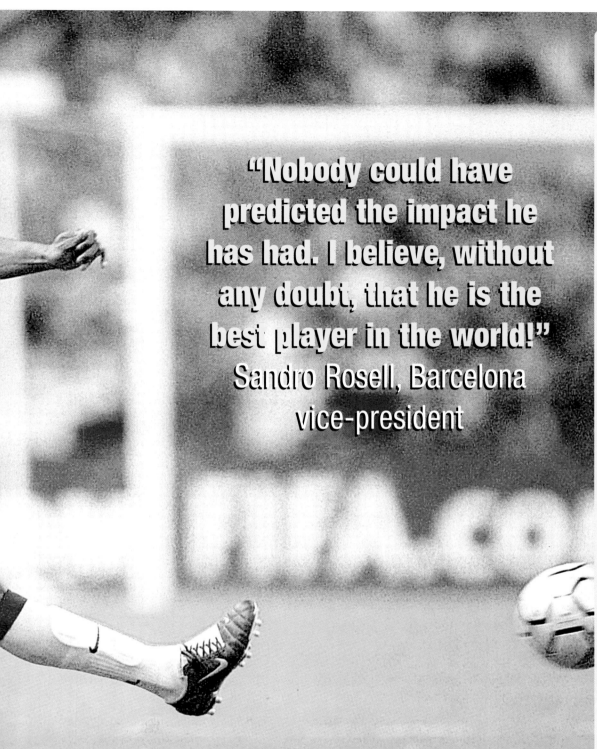

"Nobody could have predicted the impact he has had. I believe, without any doubt, that he is the best player in the world!"
Sandro Rosell, Barcelona vice-president

MATCH salutes the skills of **BARCELONA** ace **RONALDINHO**!

Brazil has a habit of churning out special footballers, but Ronaldinho could turn out to be extra-special if the first years of his career are anything to go by! Ronaldinho has become one of the best players in the world since first making an impact at Gremio, his hometown club. He then won youth honours for Brazil, moved to Paris St Germain, and helped his country to lift the 2002 World Cup. But it was his transfer to Barcelona which transformed him into a world superstar!

Ronny cost the Spanish giants £21 million and was unproven at the time in a big European league, but he was simply sensational in his debut season – playing in an attacking midfield role. And the best is definitely yet to come from the Brazil hero. As the world waits for the first £100 million footballer, it could easily be Ronaldinho – because that's how much it would cost to trigger the buy-out clause in his Barcelona contract!

The early years of Ronaldinho's career have been an amazing story – and now it's time for MATCH to give you the lowdown on how he became a midfield megastar!

CAREER FACTFILE!

Born: March 21, 1980 in Porto Alegre, Brazil

Nationality: Brazilian

Position: Midfielder

Height: 5ft 11ins

Weight: 11st 10lbs

Former clubs: Gremio, Paris St Germain

Signed: From Paris St Germain for £21 million on June 20, 2003

Barcelona debut: v Athletic Bilbao, August 30, 2003.

Barcelona games/goals: 40 games, 19 goals (August 2003 to May 2004)

Brazil caps/goals: 44 caps, 16 goals (June 1999 to July 2004)

January
JAN'S MAN!
Voted France's Player Of The Month after hitting six goals in seven games for PSG.

June
GOOD & BAD!
Scores free-kick winner v England at World Cup but then sent off.

July
WORLD WINNER!
Wins the 2002 World Cup with Brazil, playing in their final victory over Germany.

2002

December
FINE TIME!
Fined by PSG after returning late for training following a Christmas break.

July
BARÇA BOY!
Rejects Man. United to join Spanish side Barcelona in huge £21 million transfer.

2003

March
TOP 100!
Named as one of 11 greatest living footballers, announced by FIFA and chosen by Brazilian great Pele.

May
SMASH HIT!
Scores 15 league goals to inspire an improved Barça side to second place in La Liga.

June
STAYING PUT!
Misses Brazil's Copa America campaign through injury but thrills Barcelona by turning down Chelsea and agreeing new deal.

2004

1997

WORLD'S TOP TEEN!

Ronaldinho revealed his brilliant skills to the world on one of the biggest stages possible – the World Under-17 Championship. Having impressed Brazil coach Wanderley Luxemburgo with his top performances at youth and reserve-team level, he was called up to the Under-17 squad for the tournament in Egypt and took the competition by storm! Ronaldinho finished as the top goalscorer as Brazil won the whole competition. They coasted through the group stages and beat rivals Argentina in the quarter-finals, Germany in the semi-finals and then Ghana in the final. So Brazil were crowned World Under-17 champions and teenage sensation Ronaldinho was already well on his way to becoming a global superstar!

1998

GREMIO'S LOCAL HERO!

Ronaldinho's start in professional football was a familiar one. He signed for Brazilian club side Gremio, based in his home town of Porto Alegre – and the same club his brother Roberto played for before he retired from the game to become a football agent! Ronaldinho wasted little time in making his own name stand out in lights, though. He made his first-team debut for Gremio in 1998 and quickly established himself as one of Brazilian football's most exciting young attacking talents. Local lad Ronaldinho became a favourite with the club's fans, but it soon became obvious that a small club like Gremio wouldn't be able to keep hold of him as his fame spread worldwide!

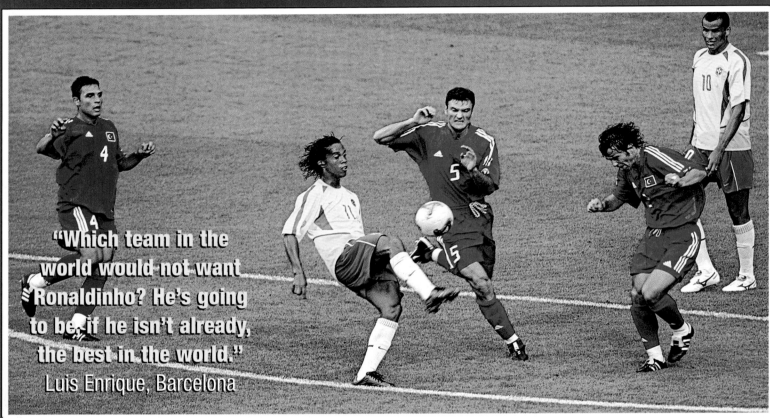

"Which team in the world would not want Ronaldinho? He's going to be, if he isn't already, the best in the world."
Luis Enrique, Barcelona

1999

SAMBA SENSATION!

Once Ronaldinho was fast-tracked into the Brazil national team in 1999, it was impossible to leave him out! The 19-year-old had a tremendous first year at senior international level, making his full debut against Latvia in June, and then squeezing into the squad for the summer's Copa America tournament in Paraguay. Brazil won the competition, and on the way to lifting the famous trophy, Ronaldinho scored a magical goal against Venezuela when he lobbed the ball over a defender, went past another and beat the goalkeeper in stunning style! He also played in the Confederations Cup in August, and although Brazil lost the final to Mexico, Ronny scored six goals – including a hat-trick in the semi-final against Saudi Arabia. It was a brilliant year for him in the Brazil team!

2001

FROM GREMIO TO PARIS!

Gremio were powerless to prevent Europe's biggest clubs from making enquiries about their young attacking star. Paris St Germain won the race to sign Ronaldinho in the end, and he was very excited about the challenge. "Every person I have met has told me it will be great," he said. "At the moment, Paris is the best place I could go. I even think every player in the world would like to play here." But the transfer was controversial and the Brazilian ace was left in limbo for months as Gremio and PSG argued over cash. Even though his contract had expired in February, Gremio still demanded a fee and the two clubs couldn't agree on one. FIFA eventually stepped in to sort the whole thing out, and Ronaldinho was finally able to play!

2002

FLUKEY FREE-KICK!

At the 2002 World Cup, Ronny was one of Brazil's key players. It was during the tournament that he became a genuine world star, probably because of the most famous goal he's ever scored in his amazing career so far. Brazil were drawing 1-1 with England when the South Americans won a free-kick 40 yards from goal. Ronaldinho was expected to send in a cross, but instead he dipped the ball over David Seaman and into the net to score the winner! "When I hit the ball, I wanted to shoot for goal – but not exactly where the ball ended up," he confessed. "I had a shot at goal and I got a little lucky. Every time I see Seaman on the television, it reminds me of that moment. I will remember it for a long time."

2002

WORLD CUP WINNER!

After beating England in the quarter-finals, Brazil were red-hot favourites to win the World Cup but had to get past Turkey in the semi-finals without Ronaldinho. He had been sent off later on in the game against England and watched the 1-0 semi-final win from the sidelines! But he was recalled to the side for the final in Yokohama, and he played a big role as Brazil overcame stubborn Germany to win 2-0 – thanks to a Ronaldo double in the second half. Brazil were the world champions once again and Ronaldinho was a World Cup winner at the age of just 22!

2002

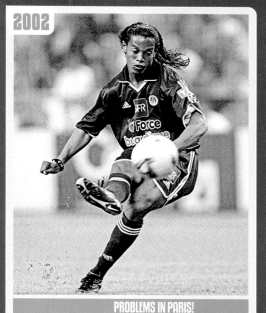

PROBLEMS IN PARIS!

After all the fuss surrounding his big move to PSG, Ronaldinho was relieved to settle down and start playing for the French club. His first season was reasonably successful, as he scored seven goals in 19 league starts – with PSG finishing fourth in the French championship – and another couple in the UEFA Cup. But things started to turn sour during his second campaign in Paris, as the Brazilian clashed with coach Luis Fernandez. "If this situation isn't resolved, one of us will have to leave," he warned. When Ronaldinho failed to turn up for a training session after Christmas 2002, giving toothache as his excuse, his days as a Paris St Germain player were numbered!

2003

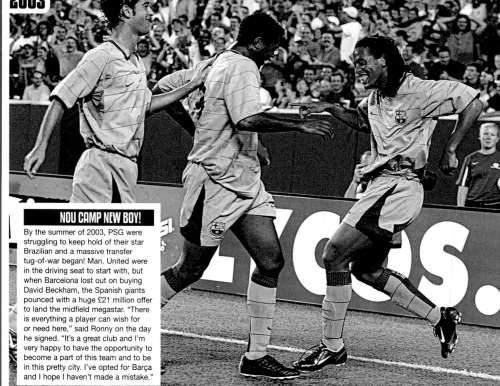

NOU CAMP NEW BOY!

By the summer of 2003, PSG were struggling to keep hold of their star Brazilian and a massive transfer tug-of-war began! Man. United were in the driving seat to start with, but when Barcelona lost out on buying David Beckham, the Spanish giants pounced with a huge £21 million offer to land the midfield megastar. "There is everything a player can wish for or need here," said Ronny on the day he signed. "It's a great club and I'm very happy to have the opportunity to become a part of this team and to be in this pretty city. I've opted for Barça and I hope I haven't made a mistake."

2004

THE KING OF BARÇA!

Ronaldinho had a big test on his hands when he joined Barcelona. They had struggled the previous season, scraping into sixth place in La Liga and only just making the UEFA Cup. They were also way behind bitter rivals Real Madrid. Barça made a slow start, but when Ronaldinho hit top gear, the team surged up the table thanks to a 19-match unbeaten run! Barcelona beat Zaragoza 3-0 on January 11 and didn't lose again until May 8 against Celta. Ronaldinho's contribution was huge. He scored 15 league goals and created many more – including a wonderful piece of skill to set up Xavi's winner against Real Madrid in April – and was the star of the team. Barça finished runners-up to Valencia and qualified for the Champions League. The Catalan club was back!

2004

FOOTBALL'S MOST WANTED!

At the end of his first season in Spain, Ronaldinho was one of the best players in the world. He had proven himself in one of Europe's toughest leagues, and produced some magical displays to make Barcelona a major force again. No wonder transfer talk went into overdrive! When Chelsea tried and failed with a reported £55 million bid, Barça increased his salary to £3.5 million, extended his deal until 2008, and increased his buyout clause to £100 million! "You know why I didn't go to Chelsea?" he said. "Because I love football and I want to play it in an attractive way." All this from a player who doesn't turn 25 until March 2005! The best is surely yet to come!

A WICKEDY WELCOME TO DA FIRST OF ME FIVE SUPER TUFF QUIZZES! GIVE 'EM YER BEST SHOT!

HELP PERCY!

I'VE MIXED UP ALL THESE SILLY PWAYER NAMES. CAN YOU FILL IN THEIR PWOPER NAMES PWEASE?

1. Wedwey Kwing — ANSWER
2. Wobert Piwes — ANSWER
3. Ferwando Towwes — ANSWER
4. Wantonio Cassanwo — ANSWER
5. Awexei Smertwin — ANSWER

2 POINTS FOR EACH CORRECT ANSWER

MY SCORE /10

RONALDINHO QUIZ!

ME AND DA SILKY SAMBA STAR RONALDINHO ARE BEZZIE MATES, BUT 'OW MUCH DO YA KNOW ABOUT 'IM?

1 Barcelona coughed up loads of cash for Ron, but exactly how much?

2 And from which wicked French team did Barca buy him in July 2003?

3 Which number does the tricky forward wear for Barcelona?

4 Which England 'keeper did he cheekily chip at the 2002 World Cup?

5 And what letter does Ronny wear on a gold chain around his neck?

2 POINTS FOR EACH CORRECT ANSWER

MY SCORE /10

CHANGIN' SHIRTS!

TWO OF THESE DUDES 'AVE SWAPPED SHIRTS BEFORE DA FINAL WHISTLE – BUT CAN YA WORK OUT WHICH TWO?

5 POINTS FOR EACH CORRECT ANSWER

MY SCORE /10

Alessandro Nesta

Wilfred Bouma

Ivan Helguera

Lilian Thuram

Olof Mellberg

John Terry

WORD SEARCH

THERE'S A LOAD OF ME BESTEST FOOTY MATES HIDIN' SOMEWHERE IN DIS GRID THINGY. CAN YA FIND 'EM ALL FOR ME?

```
R A T C R A R S C A M P B E L L Q N I E
K S Z R J S I Y R U R C E B M U V L E H
Y A K U B U R V V E R P A K O V S K I S
H G H G F N O I Q E W L L M T C T X X R
E N V E E M S E T O F O L W H Q V C U X
M M A H K G R I W M W B X J A V F Z Z D
J P X C J E P R T O M A S S O N H U R Z
L X I W A V O A E A C K P R S Z T L N C
H L D X V K G E R R A R D Y U M I A M V
K S G O K O C H A J R C O L E P M M V I
V W J O A Q U I N R O N A L D O S P Y U
H L W B L Z O L G W P L N I R F H A C T
Z P N G R O S I C K Y P U D K W E R Q U
B S N L Q O Z T C Q A Q K A X I A D U S
B K S R O O N E Y M W N Z Z Z B R B A Q
V A H T Y Z C E L L Z B E L K Q E G I S
S H R B Y H X D U F F O O H M U R T V X
Z D P O Z I H B X G Z Z P K E Y N S V C
U Q S H S V I S B A L L A C K B H F S F
```

> **Ballack**
> **Baros**
> **Campbell**
> **Cole**
> **Duff**
> **Gerrard**
> **Henry**
> **Joaquin**
> **Lampard**
> **Okocha**
> **Prso**
> **Ronaldo**
> **Rooney**
> **Rosicky**
> **Shearer**
> **Smith**
> **Tomasson**
> **Verpakovskis**
> **Vieira**
> **Yakubu**

1/2 POINT FOR EACH CORRECT ANSWER

MY SCORE /10

dream team!

THESE GEEZERS WERE WELL IMPRESSIVE AT EURO 2004, BUT CAN YA WORK OUT WHO'S WHO BY READING DA SIMPLE CLUES? GIVE IT A GO!

Denmark and Villa 'keeper!

GK

Thomas Sorensen

Portugal and Chelsea full-back!
RB
ANSWER

Latvia's ex-Arsenal defender!
CB
ANSWER

Greece's ex-Shef'ield United ace!
CB
ANSWER

Versatile Italy and Juventus star!
LB
ANSWER

Bolton and Greece speedster!
RM
ANSWER

France and Real Madrid magician!
CM
ANSWER

Dreadlocked Dutch pitbull!
CM
ANSWER

Long-haired Czech trickster!
LM
ANSWER

Swedish ace with golden boots!
S
ANSWER

Brazilian-born German striker!
S
ANSWER

1 POINT FOR EACH CORRECT ANSWER

MY SCORE /10

RUUD VAN NISTELROOY · HOLLAND

WORLD SUPER STRIKERS

WS

EURO 2004

DIARY!

THE AGONY...

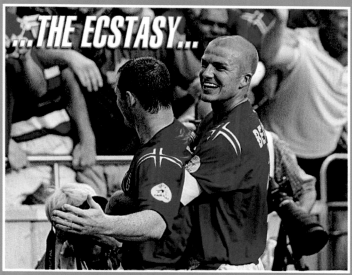

...THE ECSTASY...

...A FESTIVAL OF FOOTY!

Del Piero was one of the Italy stars who failed to shine!

At least Buffon made some top-class saves!

"Mamma mia! Italy have-a been pants again!"

TOTTI IN TROUBLE AS ITALY CRASH!

ITALY WENT INTO EURO 2004 AS ONE of the favourites to win it, but they went home early after Francesco Totti threw a wobbly! The Azzurri's attacking formation didn't pay off against Denmark in their first game, as the Danes kept possession of the ball well and defended strongly.

Italy got more and more frustrated, and Francesco Totti reacted – first by sliding in with a high tackle on Thomas Gravesen, and then by spitting in Christian Poulsen's face! The referee didn't spot the incident and the game finished 0-0. But Danish TV pictures spotted the incident and UEFA banned the Roma striker for three games, leaving Italy without their star man!

The Azzurri grabbed a 1-1 draw against Sweden in their next game, with Antonio Cassano – Totti's replacement – scoring their goal. They now needed a win, and results to go their way, in the final Group C games to reach the quarter-finals.

Italy did their bit, beating Bulgaria 2-1. But results went against them as Sweden and Denmark drew the other game 2-2, meaning the Italians were on the next plane home. Totti looked on helpless from the stands as his team crashed out early!

No.13 was unlucky for Michael Ballack!

Germany didn't even make it to the quarter-finals!

These fans were well hacked off after losing to Portugal!

The Spain stars failed to impress – again!

GERMANY AND SPAIN FALL SHORT!

NO MATTER HOW IMPRESSIVE YOUR FOOTBALL HISTORY IS, you've got to get results to stay in a tournament – that's what went wrong with Germany and Spain at Euro 2004. Rudi Voller's Germany began brightly against Holland, but Ruud van Nistelrooy's equaliser and a 1-1 final scoreline shook their confidence. Next came Latvia, who taught them a lesson, with the Germans lucky to draw 0-0. Against a weak Czech Republic side – who had already qualified for the last eight – the Germans lost 2-1 after taking the lead and the three-times winners were out!

Spain have a history of under-performing at major finals, so it was no surprise when they crashed out in the first round. Inaki Saez's men looked tired in the first match against Russia, but they still won 1-0 thanks to Juan Carlos Valeron. They were better against Greece, but Fernando Morientes's strike was only enough for a 1-1 draw. This left them needing to beat Portugal for a place in the last eight, but a 1-0 defeat broke Spanish hearts again!

"Don't worry guys – at least you haven't got grey hair like me!"

June 12 OPENING GAME SHOCKER!

There's a big shock in the opening game of Euro 2004 as Greece defeat host country Portugal 2-1 in Group A. The Portuguese fans are stunned, knowing their team now face an uphill struggle just to get out of the group. But their big rivals Spain make a promising start with a 1-0 win over Russia, as Juan Carlos Valeron comes off the bench to bag the winning goal in the 59th minute!

June 13 CRUEL BLOW FOR ENGLAND!

Switzerland and Croatia play out a boring 0-0 draw in Group B, but the big one – England v France – is next! Frank Lampard gives Sven's men the lead with a brilliant first-half header. But David Beckham misses a penalty in the second-half, and in the last two minutes of the match, Zinedine Zidane scores twice – with an expert free-kick and a penalty – to give France a 2-1 win!

June 14 IT'S FIVE-STAR SWEDEN!

Italy, who are second favourites to win the tournament, start with a disappointing 0-0 draw against Denmark. Danish 'keeper Thomas Sorensen is in great form as Italy pour forward, but the Danes almost win it, with Gigi Buffon making a fantastic double-save late on. The other Group C game is a corker, with Henrik Larsson's Sweden winning 5-0 against a poor Bulgaria side!

June 15 RUUD BOY SAVES HOLLAND!

Latvia take a surprise lead against the Czech Republic, but the highly-rated Czechs win 2-1 thanks to Marek Heinz and Milan Baros. In the other Group D match, Holland find it tough to break down a well-organised Germany side, with midfielder Torsten Frings opening the scoring with a free-kick before Ruud van Nistelrooy equalises with a brilliant volley nine minutes from time!

June 16 PORTUGAL BACK ON TRACK!

Spain start well against Greece, with Raul's clever backheel setting up Morientes. But Angelos Charisteas levels the score in the second half, and despite dazzling wing play from Vicente and Jose Etxeberria, Spain can't grab a winner. Portugal breathe a big sigh of relief as they beat Russia 2-0, with goals from Maniche and Rui Costa giving them hope of reaching the quarter-finals!

Ex-Celtic striker Henrik Larsson was quality!

"Hey, let me give you a head massage!"

"Get in – we're having fish and chips tonight!"

SWEDEN RUN OUT OF STEAM!

SWEDEN HAD A GREAT CHANCE of going all the way at Euro 2004. They won their first game in style, whupping Bulgaria 5-0, with Henrik Larsson netting one of the goals of the tournament with a fine header.

And they looked comfortable in their other Group C games against Italy and Denmark. Despite falling 1-0 behind to both countries, the Swedes battled hard to come back and score the goals that sent them through to the knockout stages.

In the quarter-finals they faced a Holland team that had only just sneaked through Group D, but Sweden didn't play at their best and failed to threaten for most of the game. It went to penalties and the smart money was on Sweden, considering Holland's terrible record from the spot. But it was the Swedes who lost their bottle, as stars Ibrahimovic and Mellberg missed their vital kicks. Sweden were out of the tournament!

Sweden crashed out on penalties!

Jesper Gronkjaer after losing to the Czechs!

Denmark's Jon Dahl Tomasson was on target against Sweden!

The Danes drew 0-0 with Italy in their first game!

But Denmark lost in the last eight to the Czechs!

DENMARK'S DREAM COMES TO AN END!

THE DANES IMPRESSED IN THEIR FIRST GAME, WITH 'KEEPER Thomas Sorensen keeping Italy out with some super saves as the match finished 0-0. Against Bulgaria, Everton's Thomas Gravesen was in superb form, out-muscling the opposition and setting up Denmark's attack on the way to a 2-0 win. In the final group game against Sweden, the pressure was on the Danes as they still weren't sure of qualifying for the quarter-finals. But striker Jon Dahl Tomasson scored twice – including a fantastic 25-yard volley – as Denmark scraped through to the last eight.

Now came the real test – could Denmark make the semi-finals and overcome a classy Czech Republic team? The Danes dominated the first half but failed to make any clear-cut chances. And just minutes after the restart, the Czechs made Denmark pay – scoring three times in a 16-minute spell through Jan Koller and a Milan Baros brace. After that early promise, it wasn't to be for Denmark!

EURO 2004
DIARY OF A TOURNAMENT

Michael Owen opened the scoring against Portugal!

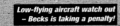

Frank Lampard took the game to penalties!

Low-flying aircraft watch out – Becks is taking a penalty!

Paul Scholes scored against Croatia!

"Quick, let's get out of here Darius!"

ENGLAND'S PENALTY PAIN!

ENGLAND MADE IT 38 PAINFUL YEARS WITHOUT A TROPHY – and continued their shocking luck in penalty shoot-outs – as Sven Goran Eriksson's men crashed out in the quarter-finals of Euro 2004. It had looked so good early on. Only two injury-time Zinedine Zidane goals and a missed David Beckham penalty stopped England from beating France in the first game, before they smashed Switzerland 3-0 and Croatia 4-2 to book a place in the quarter-finals.

Then came Portugal. England got off to a great start when Michael Owen scored after just three minutes, but it went badly wrong when Wayne Rooney went off injured. The Three Lions tried to keep their lead, but they conceded an equaliser with just seven minutes left on the clock. They might have nicked it when Sol Campbell scored in injury-time, but the goal was disallowed and it went to extra-time. Portugal scored, before Frank Lampard hit back for Sven's men, so it went to penalties. Becks sent his spot-kick into space and Darius Vassell saw his effort saved in sudden death. England were out!

England took the lead against France!

A Rooney rocket beat Croatia in Group B!

Stevie G grabbed the third goal against Switzerland!

WAYNE'S WORLD!

IF EUROPE DIDN'T KNOW HOW GOOD Wayne Rooney was before Euro 2004, they soon found out! From the first game against France, Roonaldo upset defenders with his pace, power and trickery – winning a penalty in the 2-1 defeat. In the second game against Switzerland he hit two goals in a Man Of The Match display, and two more strikes followed in a Man Of The Match show against Croatia!

Against Portugal in the semi-finals, England lost their way after Rooney hobbled off injured, showing how important he had become to the national team. In the space of just a month he'd become a superstar, with a £50 million price tag on his head and all the world's top clubs after him. 'Roo-mania' had arrived.

June 17 SWISS ROLL FOR ENGLAND!

England get a big boost with a 3-0 win over Switzerland and a Man Of The Match display from Wayne Rooney! The 18-year-old opens the scoring with a simple header, and then makes it 2-0 with a second-half thunderbolt, before Stevie Gerrard wraps up the win near the end! Croatia hold France to a 2-2 draw and even miss a great chance to win the game in the last minute!

June 18 TOTTI TROUBLE FOR ITALY!

Bulgaria lose their second game and have captain Stilian Petrov sent off for arguing as they fall 2-0 to Denmark. Italy, without Francesco Totti – who is suspended after a spitting incident in the Denmark match – can only draw with Sweden. They dominate the game and lead through Antonio Cassano, but Zlatan Ibrahimovic gets a dramatic late equaliser with a jumping backheel!

June 19 CZECH MATES GO THROUGH!

Latvia play out of their skins and hold Germany to a 0-0 draw, leaving Group D wide open. The Czech Republic come back from 2-0 down against Holland to win 3-2 in the game of the tournament so far! The Czechs throw everything into attack and goals from Koller and Baros make it 2-2. In the 88th minute, Vladimir Smicer finishes a great move to send his team into the quarter-finals!

June 20 UNLUCKY SPAIN CRASH OUT!

It's crunch time for the hosts, who need a win against Spain to qualify for the quarter-finals. Roared on by their fans, Portugal come out fighting, and Nuno Gomes puts them in front, drilling in a shot from 25 yards. Fernando Torres hits the woodwork twice for Spain, but they run out of ideas and crash out of the tournament. Greece join Portugal in the next round, despite losing 2-1 to Russia!

June 21 ROONEY MANIA STRIKES!

England need three points to qualify for the quarter-finals, but Croatia take the lead following a free-kick. That shocks Sven's men into action – Paul Scholes equalises and Wayne Rooney scores two fantastic goals to put England 3-1 up! Croatia get one back, but Frank Lampard ends the contest with a fourth goal! France also make the last eight, beating Switzerland 3-1!

Henry and Zidane were both gutted after losing to Greece!

FRANCE FALL!

HOLDERS FRANCE WENT INTO EURO 2004 as hot favourites to keep their title, after going through qualifying without dropping a point – but they ended up looking like chumps!

Jacques Santini's side didn't look focused from the start, needing two injury-time goals to scrape past England in the opening game. Next up was a 2-2 draw with Croatia, where they were 2-1 down at one point, before they rallied to beat a poor Switzerland side 3-1.

The warning signs were there for all to see. Thierry Henry hadn't been the player who had rocked the Premiership all season, Zinedine Zidane was nowhere near his sensational best, and there were question marks over the defence. But they were still expected to easily beat Greece – who had never won a game at a major finals before Euro 2004.

But that wasn't the case, and a lacklustre France were out-fought and out-thought by Greece, who delivered one of footy's biggest shocks when Angelos Charisteas's header sent the French home in embarrassment!

David James gave away a penalty against France!

Zizou curled in a wicked free-kick against England!

David Trezeguet scored against Croatia!

"Which one of you lot called me baldy?"

ZZ'S SPOT-KICK SICKENER!

WHILE ENGLAND WERE SICK OF PENALTIES AFTER EURO 2004, Zinedine Zidane was actually sick while taking one! The barf-o-rama happened at the end of France's game with England. Zizou had just scored an injury-time free-kick to make it 1-1 when Thierry Henry was fouled in the area. The referee pointed to the spot, and France had the chance to win a game they'd never looked like winning!

Zidane stepped up, but after placing the ball down on the spot, his nerves suddenly got the better of him. He hunched over, put his hands on his knees, took a deep breath – and spewed up all over the pitch! But before anyone could say 'Sacre Bleugh!' the France captain had smashed the ball into the back of the net to give his country a dramatic 2-1 win. Sickening, just sickening!

Henry asked the ref if he could go to the loo!

Marek Heinz scored the winner against Latvia!

'Czech' these guys out – they're slammin'!

UEFA didn't let Jan Koller steal the corner flag!

CZECHS CHOKE IN THE SEMIS!

THE CZECH REPUBLIC HEADED INTO EURO 2004 WITH THE TAG OF 'DARK horses' – a team that could surprise some of the so-called bigger sides and go on to win the tournament. And they nearly did! The Czechs played some brilliant stuff, and as the competition moved into the final week, they won a new army of neutral fans who were impressed by their all-out attacking style!

After surviving an early scare – they were trailing to Latvia before coming back to win 2-1 – the Czechs developed a habit of coming from behind to win games. They were 2-0 down to Holland but came back to win 3-2, and were 1-0 down to Germany before winning 2-1. The Czechs seemed to be invincible, especially after thrashing an in-form Denmark side 3-0 in the quarter-finals!

In the semi-final against Greece, they were red-hot favourites to win the match and make the final. But the loss of star playmaker Pavel Nedved before half-time hurt their chances and the Greeks won the game with a Silver Goal in extra-time. **"It will take a long time to come to terms with this,"** said Nedved afterwards. **"Yet this is the best team I've ever played in. We have a real team spirit."**

Pavel Nedved won the silly hair competition!

Milan Baros thought the Czechs would make the final!

"98, 99, 100! I'm coming to find you guys!"

BAROS HAS GOLDEN BOOTS!

MILAN BAROS WENT INTO EURO 2004 AS A LIVERPOOL reserve, but he ended it as the tournament's top goalscorer and a transfer target for Real Madrid and Barcelona! Baros was sensational, scoring five goals to win the Golden Boot. His first was a crucial equaliser against Latvia, and then he volleyed home a super strike in the thriller against Holland.

The Czech striker was rested for the third match against Germany, but he came off the bench in the second half to race clear and slot home the winner. In the quarter-final with Denmark, Baros struck twice more. One was a neat chip and the other a fierce blast. That made it five goals in four games, and although he drew a blank in the semi-final loss to Greece, Baros finished as the top scorer to win the Golden Boot!

June 22 ITALY GO HOME DESPITE WIN!

In the final games of Group C, two from Italy, Denmark or Sweden can still make the quarter-finals. The Italians only just scrape a win against Bulgaria thanks to Antonio Cassano's 90th-minute winner, but it isn't enough as Denmark and Sweden get a point each in a 2-2 draw and both of them go through. The Italians, tipped by many to reach the final, crash out on goal difference!

June 23 HOLLAND THANK GERMANY!

With the Czech Republic already through, the other quarter-final spot is still between Germany, Holland and Latvia going into the last game of Group D. Latvia have done well so far, but Holland are simply too good for them – with two goals from Ruud van Nistelrooy and one from Roy Makaay. The Czech Republic beat Germany 2-1 in the other game, sending Holland through!

June 24 ENGLAND'S PENALTY HELL!

In the quarter-final between Portugal and England, Michael Owen opens the scoring after three minutes, but Wayne Rooney hobbles off midway through the first-half. Portugal equalise, but a last-gasp Sol Campbell goal is ruled out before the game goes to extra-time and ends 2-2. David Beckham and Darius Vassell miss in the penalty shoot-out and England's campaign is over!

June 25 FRANCE'S GREEK TRAGEDY!

Greece shock the world by knocking out favourites France in the second quarter-final. In the 64th minute, Angelos Charisteas jumps unmarked to score with a powerful header and the Greek fans go berserk! France throw on Louis Saha, Sylvain Wiltord and Jerome Rothen in a desperate bid to score an equaliser, but there's no way past the impressive Greece defence!

June 26 HOLLAND INTO THE SEMIS!

Everyone expects goals galore as Sweden take on Holland, but the game ends 0-0 after extra-time and it's decided on a penalty shoot-out! The Dutch have a shocking record with spot-kicks, and it looks like more pain when Phillip Cocu misses. But Zlatan Ibrahimovic and Olof Mellberg miss for Sweden, and Arjen Robben scores the winning penalty after a dazzling performance!

Arjen Robben scored the vital spot-kick against Sweden!

Holland's warm-up routine was a bit strange!

Ruud van Nistelrooy scored four goals!

The Dutch fell at the semi-final stage again!

MORE HEARTBREAK FOR HOLLAND!

HOLLAND'S HOPES ENDED IN THE SAME WAY AS THEIR LAST two tournaments – with a defeat in the semi-finals. The Dutch have developed a habit of falling in the last four. They lost in the semis of the 1998 World Cup, in the semis of Euro 2000, and they crashed out of the semis at Euro 2004 by losing 2-1 to hosts Portugal!

But the team probably did better than expected. Against Germany they needed a late Ruud van Nistelrooy equaliser to rescue a point, and they blew a 2-0 lead in the next game against the Czechs. But a 3-0 win over Latvia sent them through to the quarter-finals, where they faced a strong Sweden side.

After 120 minutes of goalless action, the game went to penalties, which filled the Dutch with dread. Their record from the spot over the years was poor, but Holland managed to nail their hoodoo when new Chelsea star Arjen Robben scored in sudden death to send them through!

Dutch hopes had been raised, but their luck ran out in the semi-finals. Were they unlucky? Maybe, but the only team they managed to beat in 90 minutes was Latvia!

Ronaldo went to give his United team-mate a hug!

HOLLAND 2 CZECH REPUBLIC 3!

THE GAME OF THE TOURNAMENT WAS THE FANTASTIC GROUP match between Holland and the Czech Republic – it was an end-to-end classic! The Dutch started on fire when defender Wilfred Bouma headed them in front after four minutes. And with Chelsea-bound winger Arjen Robben enjoying loads of possession, the Oranje extended their lead on 19 minutes when Ruud van Nistelrooy finished off Robben's cross.

But the Czechs pulled a goal back within minutes when Jan Koller converted a Milan Baros cross. Edgar Davids hit the post for Holland, but when Johnny Heitinga was sent off in the second half, the game swung in favour of the Czechs. Baros's sensational volley made it 2-2, but with Holland hanging on desperately for a draw, Vladimir Smicer grabbed the winner! This game had everything – two attacking teams, shots against the bar, five great goals and a red card. Fantastic!

"Sniff, is that me? Oh man, it is – I'm humming today!"

EURO 2004
DIARY OF A TOURNAMENT

Veteran star Rui Costa showed he's still class!

Euro 2004 was full of highs and lows for Portugal!

Postiga came off the bench to score against England!

PORTUGAL'S FINAL FLING!

EURO 2004 PRODUCED SO MANY UPS AND DOWNS for host country Portugal. For their Golden Generation of senior players like Luis Figo, Rui Costa and Fernando Couto, this tournament was seen as their last chance of winning a trophy – and in front of their own fans too!

But after losing their first match to Greece, Couto and Rui Costa were dropped from the starting XI, and wins over Russia, Spain, England and Holland saw them into the final. Despite home advantage and 65,000 screaming fans in the Luz Stadium, Greece won 1-0 as Portugal's fairytale quickly turned into a nightmare. They'll never have a better chance of winning their first major trophy!

Cristiano Ronaldo was in tears...

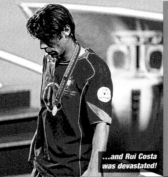

...and Rui Costa was devastated!

Portugal had a real spring in their step!

"Look girls – I've been working out!"

Maniche scored a cracker in the semi against Holland!

FANTASTIC FANS!

AS PORTUGAL MARCHED TO THE EURO 2004 final, their fans painted a sea of red and green at every game and stadium! From waving their scarves madly to painting their faces and screaming for their country, the atmosphere created by the Portugal fans made the tournament brilliant to watch. They were all shedding tears when they lost the final to Greece in Lisbon, but even neutral fans will remember how they lit up the tournament for three fantastic weeks!

Felipe Scolari was an inspirational coach!

June 27 BAROS DESTROYS DENMARK!

The much-admired Czech Republic take on Denmark in the last quarter-final, but the Danes dominate the first half. After the break, the Czechs score three goals in 16 minutes thanks to the free running of Karel Poborsky and captain Pavel Nedved. Jan Koller grabs the first, then Milan Baros scores his fourth and fifth goals of the competition to set up a semi-final meeting with Greece!

June 30 FINAL JOY FOR PORTUGAL!

With France, England and Italy out, Holland fancy their chances of getting to the Euro 2004 final. Portugal are the better side for most of this semi-final though, and they go 2-0 ahead through a simple Ronaldo header and a rocket from Maniche, who strikes after a quick corner. Holland come back into it thanks to an Andrade own goal, but the hosts hold their nerve to finish 2-1 winners!

July 1 CZECH REPUBLIC DREAM ENDS!

Greece are full of confidence for their semi-final with the Czech Republic, but they get an early scare when Tomas Rosicky smashes the crossbar. The game swings in their favour when Pavel Nedved is forced off through injury, but it ends goalless and goes into extra-time. Greece dominate, and in the last second of the first half, Traianos Dellas heads his side into the Euro 2004 final!

July 4 GREEK GODS LIFT THE TROPHY!

There's a wicked atmosphere for the final in the Estadio da Luz, but Portugal look nervous in front of their flag-waving fans. Deco, Figo and Ronaldo all try their magic, but Angelos Charisteas scores the winning goal from a 57th-minute corner to spark wild celebrations! Before Euro 2004, Greece had never won a single game at a tournament – this time they won the whole competition!

UEFA Euro 2004™
GREECE CHAMPIONS

Greece were crowned Euro 2004 champions!

GREECE IS THE WORD!

The players went crazy after beating Portugal in the final!

GREECE CAME INTO EURO 2004 HAVING NEVER won a single game in a major tournament. But after lifting the trophy in one of footy's biggest-ever shocks, they were the team everyone was talking about!

From their 2-1 win over hosts Portugal in the opening game to dumping out France, the Czech Republic and Portugal again in the final, they proved to be the best team in the competition. Built on a fantastic defence that only conceded four goals in the whole tournament, and playing a highly-effective counter-attacking game, the Greeks frustrated and surprised the so-called 'big' teams and powered their way to glory in Lisbon.

Despite not having any megastars or a coach with a seven-figure salary, their confidence, class and ability saw them crowned European champions. Go Greece!

All the players wanted to get their hands on the trophy...

...but they struggled to get it from Dellas!

CAPTAIN FANTASTIC!

WHAT A FAIRYTALE EURO 2004 WAS FOR THEO Zagorakis. The 32-year-old midfielder spent two years at Leicester from 1998 to 2000, but he struggled to get a game in the Premiership and joined AEK Athens on a free transfer. After playing in all eight of Greece's Euro 2004 qualifiers, Zagorakis captained his country at the finals and impressed with his work-rate, vision and leadership. In the final against Portugal he was one of the best players on the pitch, as the Greeks held off the hosts to win 1-0. And not only did Theo have the honour of lifting the trophy for his nation, he was also named UEFA's Player Of The Tournament!

DID YOU KNOW...?
EVEN THOUGH PLAYERS LIKE IAN WALKER, JOE COLE AND WAYNE BRIDGE DIDN'T KICK A BALL AT EURO 2004, THEY STILL GOT £100,000 EACH FROM THE FA JUST FOR TRAVELLING TO PORTUGAL! YOWSERS!

> I'LL STICK IT IN MY PIGGY BANK! OINK!

> WICKED! I MIGHT BUY A NEW TRAIN SET!

My Fave...

CD ★ Jagged Edge

My Fave...

BABE ★ My girlfriend

My Fave...

FILM ★ Good Will Hunting

My Fave...

TV SHOW ★ 24

My Fave...

FOOD ★ Italian

My Favourite Things!

Name: Owen Hargreaves
Age: 23
Club: Bayern Munich

My Fave...

CAR ★ Audi RS6

My Fave...
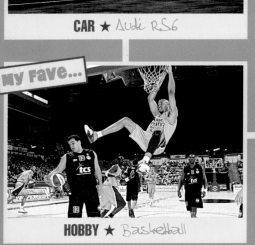
HOBBY ★ Basketball

PREMIERSHIP PLAYER ★ Thierry Henry

My Fave...

HOLIDAY ★ Mali

My Fave...

ANIMAL ★ Dog

WORLD SUPER STRIKERS

WS

DJIBRIL CISSE · LIVERPOOL

MATCHMAN'S QUIZ!

HERE'S ME SECOND TUFF QUIZ, FOOTY DUDES AND DUDETTES! 'OW ARE YA DOIN' SO FAR?

YEARBOOK QUESTIONS
PROFILES
FOOTY STATS
LEAGUE
STATTOS

PERCY'S TWUE OR FALSE!

HEWWO EVERYONE! PUT A TICK IN THE BOX FOR COWWECT FOOTBALL FACTS, AND A CWOSS FOR INCOWWECT ONES!

1. David Beckham wears 22 for Weal Madwid!
2. James Beattie used to pway for Blackburn!
3. Gawy Neville is older than Phil Neville!
4. Swen Gowan Eriksson is from Norway!
5. Les Ferdinand is Wio Ferdinand's daddy!

2 POINTS FOR EACH CORRECT ANSWER   **MY SCORE /10**

TRANSFER TRACKER!

DUTCH DUDE SEEDORF 'AS PLAYED FER LOADS OF TOP CLUBS, BUT DO YA KNOW WHICH ONES ARE MISSIN'?

Ajax	1990-1995	Ajax
	Ajax	
Sampdoria	1995-1997	
	Sampdoria	
?	1997-2000	?
?	2000-2002	?
	2002	
	AC Milan	

5 POINTS FOR EACH CORRECT ANSWER   **MY SCORE /10**

SPOT THE DIFFERENCE!

DIS IS WELL SIMPLE! JUST CIRCLE DA FIVE DIFFERENCES IN DA TWO PICTURES!

2 POINTS FOR EACH CORRECT ANSWER   **MY SCORE /10**

WHO AM I?

CAN YA FIGURE OUT WHICH WICKEDY PLAYER IS HIDIN' UNDER DA FACE OF YOURS TRULY?

> I wear number 10 for Italy!
> I also play for Roma!
> I was banned for three matches at Euro 2004 for spitting at an opponent!

10 POINTS FOR CORRECT ANSWER   **MY SCORE /10**

ULTIMATE CHALLENGE!

RIGHT GEEZERS AND GEEZETTES, IT'S TIME TO GET YER FOOTY FINKIN' CAPS ON! SEE IF YA CAN GET TEN OUT OF TEN ON ME SOLID ULTIMATE CHALLENGE!

1 Who is the ex-Valencia gaffer who replaced Gerard Houllier as Liverpool boss in the summer?

2 Which Portugal and ex-Tottenham striker scored against England at Euro 2004?

3 Which team will soon be leaving Highbury to play at a brand new stadium?

4 Which Italian team have taken Chelsea's Juan Sebastian Veron on a season-long loan?

5 Who was in charge of the England team before Sven Goran Eriksson took over?

6 Kieron Dyer has his nickname stitched into his boots – but what is it?

7 Which national team does tough-tackling midfield general Thomas Gravesen play for?

8 Which Premiership team, who play their home games at Selhurst Park, are nicknamed The Eagles?

9 Which of these top strikers is the oldest – Mikael Forssell or Emile Heskey?

10 Arsenal's skilful trickster David Bentley is on loan at which Premiership team?

1 POINT FOR EACH CORRECT ANSWER   **MY SCORE /10**

WORLD SUPER STRIKERS

WSS

THIERRY HENRY · FRANCE

MIDFIELD MEGASTARS!

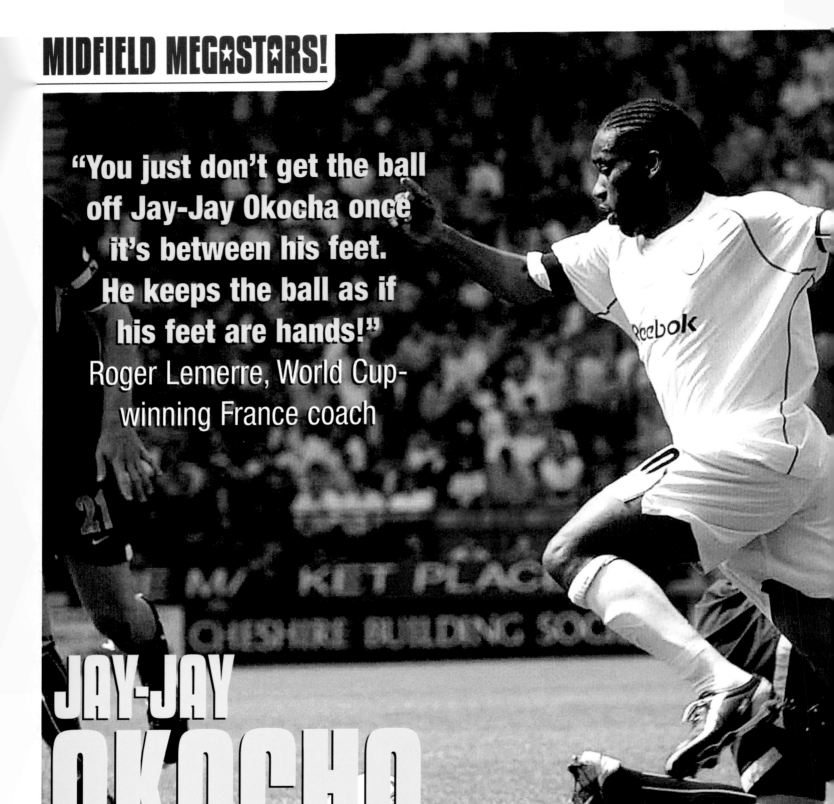

"You just don't get the ball off Jay-Jay Okocha once it's between his feet. He keeps the ball as if his feet are hands!"
Roger Lemerre, World Cup-winning France coach

JAY-JAY OKOCHA

Okocha Timeline...

May
EARLY START!
Begins playing career as a 16-year-old with Rangers International in Nigeria.

1989

July
HOLIDAY JOB!
Signs for German Division Three side Borussia Neunkirchen after a holiday in the country.

1991

August
BIG CHANCE!
Moves to the Bundesliga with one of Germany's biggest clubs, Eintracht Frankfurt.

1992

January
NATIONAL CALL-UP!
Makes his debut for the Nigeria Under-19 side – facing Cameroon in the African Youth Championship.

1993

May
NIGERIA DEBUT!
Wins first full international cap in a World Cup qualifier against the Ivory Coast. Nigeria lose 2-1.

April
EAGLES FLY HIGH!
Wins the 1994 African Nations Cup with Nigeria.

June
WORLD CUP DEBUT!
Plays three times at the 1994 World Cup as Nigeria reach the second round.

1994

August
GOLDEN BOY!
Wins Olympic Gold after beating Argentina.

HOT TURKEY!
Joins Fenerbahce for £1 million.

October
RECORD BREAKER!
Plays for Fenerbahce in an historic win at Old Trafford which ends Man. United's unbeaten home record in Europe.

1996

MATCH charts the career of BOLTON star JAY-JAY OKOCHA!

Augustine Okocha was born on August 14, 1973 in Enugu, Nigeria. He learnt his football skills on the streets before joining local clubs and moving to Nigeria's capital, Lagos, to make his name. Since then, Augustine has become known to fans as Jay-Jay – one of the most talented players in the world!

The Nigerian trickster has never won a league title or seriously challenged for a European trophy. So what makes him a midfield megastar? Well, Jay-Jay doesn't need flash team-mates or a big collection of trophies to make him a huge talent – his ability speaks for itself. He's challenged for the league title in Germany, Turkey and France, and won the African Nations Cup and the Olympic title with Nigeria. In 1998, he became Africa's most expensive footballer ever when PSG bought him for a whopping £10 million!

Now at Premiership side Bolton, Okocha is always worth paying to watch, no matter who you support! But how did he make it to the top? MATCH checks out the amazing career of the midfield megastar!

CAREER FACTFILE!

Born: August 14, 1973 in Enugu, Nigeria

Nationality: Nigerian

Position: Midfielder

Height: 5ft 8ins

Weight: 11st 0lbs

Former clubs: Rangers International, Borussia Neunkirchen, Eintracht Frankfurt, Fenerbahce, Paris St. Germain

Signed: From PSG on a free transfer on June 18, 2002

Bolton debut: v Fulham on August 17, 2002

Bolton games/goals: 73 games, 10 goals (August 2002 to May 2004)

Nigeria caps/goals: 59 games, 8 goals (May 1993 to July 2004)

July
PSG PAY UP!
Becomes the most expensive African player ever when Paris Saint Germain sign him for £10 million.

1998

August
BORDEAUX BULLDOZED!
Scores an incredible goal against Bordeaux on his PSG debut.

F.C. GIRONDINS DE BORDEAUX

2000

February
FINAL GOAL!
Scores three goals in five games at the African Nations Cup, including an equaliser in the final. But Nigeria finish runners-up behind Cameroon.

July
BOLTON BOUND!
Signs for Bolton on a free transfer after leaving PSG.

THIRD WORLD CUP!
Becomes the first Nigerian player to appear in three World Cup finals when he captains The Super Eagles in South Korea & Japan.

2002

April
CRUCIAL WIN!
Grabs the winner against relegation rivals West Ham to push Bolton towards Premiership safety.

2003

February
CONTINENT'S KEY MAN!
Wins the Most Valuable Player award at the 2004 African Nations Cup.

2004

March
CARLING CUP DEFEAT!
Picks up a Carling Cup runners-up medal after losing to Middlesbrough at the Millennium Stadium.

1992

FANTASTIC FOR FRANKFURT!

Unlike many of his future Nigeria team-mates, the talented Jay-Jay wasn't picked up by a big Dutch or French club. He signed his first contract with local Nigerian team Rangers International when he was 16 years old. It wasn't long before clubs in Europe started to take notice of his outrageous skill, but it was a small German Division Three side – Borussia Neunkirchen – who bought him to Europe after he impressed them while on holiday! Okocha dazzled in the German lower leagues for a year, before Bundesliga title challengers Eintracht Frankfurt came in to snatch the teenage sensation away. Now in a top league with a top club, he started quietly with Frankfurt, but things really took off after he scored one of the best goals in German footy history! He ran the length of the pitch in a game against Karlsruhe, before twice beating Oliver Kahn and thumping the ball into the back of the net. Jay-Jay was on the big stage, and the whole of Germany knew it!

1994

SUPER-DUPER EAGLES!

In 1994, everything was going well for Okocha in his club football. He settled well in Germany with Eintracht Frankfurt and was a key member of the team as they chased the Bundesliga title. But his international career was going nowhere fast, and the situation wasn't helped by the Nigeria coach, Clemens Westerhof. Westerhof's team was built on discipline and hard work, and he hated the tricks and turns of the exciting Okocha. As a result, the 20-year-old star wasn't selected to play in the first four games of the African Nations Cup in 1994. With Jay-Jay on the bench, Nigeria looked short of ideas, and even though the team qualified for the semi-finals, the fans demanded that their rising star was put back in the team – and they succeeded. Okocha started the semi-final, and Nigeria's flair and skill returned as they edged out the Ivory Coast on penalties. In the final against Zambia, he used his full range of tricks and flicks, carving open the opposition with his runs and dummies. Nigeria won 2-1 to lift the trophy and Okocha was named Man Of The Match. What a turnaround!

1994

WORLD CUP DEBUT!

For the 1994 World Cup in the USA, Nigeria were full of confidence, having been crowned champions of Africa just two months earlier. But despite his growing influence on the team, Clemens Westerhof again started with Okocha on the bench. This didn't worry Jay-Jay though – he came on as a substitute and mesmerised the crowd with superb cross-field passes, mazy runs and awesome tricks. In the second round against Italy, Jay-Jay was back in the starting line-up and played the full 90 minutes as Nigeria lost 2-1 in extra-time. The Nigerian team crashed out, but because of his exciting skills, Okocha's name was on everyone's lips for months afterwards!

1996

GOING FOR GOLD!

Nigeria went into the Atlanta Olympics on a poor run of form after losing to a Togo Under-23 side on home soil. So with the team looking below their best, little was expected of them at the Olympics. But they finished runners-up in their group, and in the knock-out stages, the Africans showed their true class – with Okocha's skills opening up Mexico's defence in a 2-0 win. Next up were Olympic favourites Brazil, who had already beaten Nigeria in the group stages. The challenge didn't faze The Super Eagles though, and an amazing match finished 4-3 – with Nigeria scoring a dramatic Golden Goal winner. Jay-Jay faced the biggest game of his life in the final against Argentina. It was another thriller, and Nigeria won 3-2 to lift their first football Gold at the Olympics. Okocha was on top of the world!

1996

TURKISH DELIGHT!

After his success at the Olympics, and four years spent entertaining the crowds at Frankfurt, Jay-Jay decided it was time for a new challenge. Some of the biggest clubs in Europe tried to sign him, but the ace playmaker chose Turkish champions Fenerbahce, who snapped him up for a bargain £1 million. The pressure was on him straight away as the Fenerbahce fans expected big things from the gifted Nigerian. But Jay-Jay delivered, scoring 16 goals from his attacking midfield position and impressing with his super skills in the centre of the pitch. It was a stunning first season in Turkey for Okocha, and although he didn't win a trophy, Fenerbahce finished third in the league.

1996

UNITED FALL!

Up to October 1996, Man. United had gone 30 years without losing a single European game at home. It was an unbelievable record and Old Trafford had become a real fortress of a stadium, capable of striking fear into visiting teams. So Jay-Jay Okocha's first game in England was a real challenge. His Fenerbahce team came into the match on the back of a poor run of form. They had already lost 2-0 to United two weeks earlier in Turkey, and they hadn't won in Europe in their last four games. It wasn't a classic contest, but the game sprang into life in the 79th minute – when Elvir Bolic's long-range strike was deflected in past Man. United 'keeper Peter Schmeichel. The goal silenced the 52,000 fans in Old Trafford, and the 1-0 final result stunned manager Sir Alex Ferguson, but Okocha played his part in ending one of the best home records in the history of European football! It was the first time Okocha had played in England; but it wasn't the last time he would show off his tricks at Old Trafford!

1998

PSG PAY UP!

After some dazzling displays at the France '98 World Cup, Paris Saint Germain made Okocha the most expensive African player ever when they paid Fenerbahce £10 million for the 24-year-old. Jay-Jay impressed French fans in the World Cup, beating Spain and Bulgaria before Nigeria were knocked out in the second round by Denmark. PSG hoped Okocha could inspire their stuttering side in the race for the French league title. And he didn't disappoint in his first game – smashing home a stunning 30-yard goal to sink Bordeaux! After that, the Nigeria star continued to produce flashes of magic, but he often found the going tough. Was the pressure of being Africa's most expensive player getting too much?

2000

FINAL FRUSTRATION!

The 2000 African Nations Cup was held in Nigeria, and The Super Eagles went into the tournament with probably their strongest-ever team. Okocha captained a side that boasted players from all of Europe's leading leagues – including Arsenal star Kanu, Milan defender Taribo West and George Finidi of Real Betis. The Nigerians topped their group with two wins and a draw to qualify for the knockout stages. In the quarter-finals and the semi-finals, the home crowd got behind the team as they edged past Senegal and South Africa to set up a final against Cameroon. And Jay-Jay – who had scored two goals in the group stages against Tunisia – stole the show, scoring one and setting up the other in a 2-2 draw. But with the score still level after extra-time, the game went to penalties and Nigeria's luck ran out. Cameroon won and Okocha was denied the chance to collect the trophy in Nigeria's national stadium!

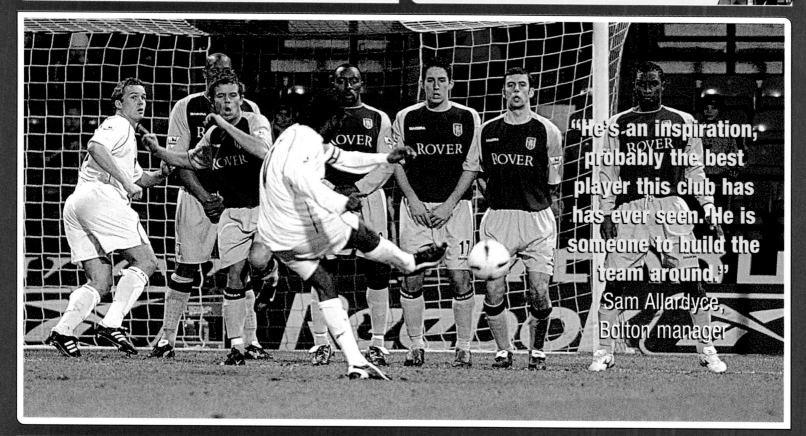

> "He's an inspiration; probably the best player this club has has ever seen. He is someone to build the team around."
> Sam Allardyce, Bolton manager

2002

BOLTON BOY!

The Nigerian ace had always wanted to play in England one day, and his dream came true in 2002. After seeing out his contract at PSG in France, he started looking for another club, and Bolton boss Sam Allardyce swooped to sign the midfield megastar before any other Premiership clubs got a sniff. Even better for Big Sam, and to the shock of other clubs, he signed on a free transfer! The Trotters had only just avoided relegation in the season before he arrived. But with Jay-Jay strutting his stuff on the pitch, Bolton fans were soon treated to attractive, attacking football as Okocha linked up with Youri Djorkaeff, Ivan Campo and Kevin Nolan. Bolton still struggled in his first campaign – finishing in 17th place – but his world-class talent would give them a new dimension in his second season!

2004

CARLING CUP FINAL!

In 2004, Okocha led Nigeria to third place at the African Nations Cup and was named Player Of The Tournament after scoring four goals in six games! Before he left for the tournament, he scored twice in the first leg of Bolton's Carling Cup semi-final against Aston Villa – putting his side ahead inside two minutes and making the game safe with an unstoppable free-kick as The Trotters won 5-2. Jay-Jay was away with Nigeria for the second leg, which Bolton lost 2-0, but they still made it through to the final with Middlesbrough – and Okocha was back for that one! He couldn't inspire The Trotters to the trophy at The Millennium Stadium, but he'd more than played his part in helping them to the final – and finishing eighth in the Premiership! And there's more to come from Jay-Jay Okocha. We can't wait!

PENALTY KINGS!

5 PENALTY KINGS!

1 RICARDO **PORTUGAL**

2 DIDA **BRAZIL**

3 EDWIN VAN DER SAR **HOLLAND**

4 FABIEN BARTHEZ **FRANCE**

5 GIGI BUFFON **ITALY**

DR. FOOTY'S SURGERY! HOW TO...

SAVE PENALTIES!

HI, I'M DOCTOR FOOTY, AND I'M GOING TO HELP YOU BECOME A SUPER SPOT-KICK STOPPER!

2

PENALTY FACT!
Eight penalties were awarded during normal time at Euro 2004, and only one was missed – Becks against France!

4

7

3

6

I'M REALLY GLAD I LISTENED TO DR. FOOTY!

1

THE FAKE! **5**

PENALTY FACT!
The record number of penalty misses in one match was by Martin Palermo. He missed three times for Argentina in their 1999 Copa America clash with Colombia!

I DON'T EVEN NEED THESE GLOVES!

FOLLOW THESE SIMPLE STEPS AND YOU WILL BE TOTALLY UNBEATABLE FROM THE PENALTY SPOT IN NO TIME AT ALL!

1 CONFIDENCE!
"IN A PENALTY SHOOT-OUT, YOU ARE IN A NO-LOSE SITUATION, BECAUSE YOU'RE NOT EXPECTED TO SAVE THE SPOT-KICK. THIS SHOULD HELP YOU TO RELAX AND FOCUS."

2 MAKE YOURSELF BIG!
"NEXT, MAKE YOURSELF LOOK AS BIG AS POSSIBLE IN THE GOAL BY STANDING UP STRAIGHT AND SPREADING YOUR ARMS OUT AS WIDE AS POSSIBLE. THIS WILL MAKE THE GOAL APPEAR SMALLER TO THE PENALTY TAKER, WHICH MAY HAVE A NEGATIVE EFFECT ON HIS CONFIDENCE."

3 MOVE AROUND!
"MOVE LEFT AND RIGHT ALONG YOUR LINE. THIS MAKES IT SEEM LIKE THERE'S LESS SPACE FOR THE TAKER TO AIM FOR. BUT REMEMBER, YOU CAN'T MOVE OFF YOUR LINE YET!"

4 MAKE A DECISION!
"YOU MUST DECIDE WHETHER TO DIVE AS THE BALL IS BEING KICKED - OR REACT AFTER IT'S BEEN KICKED. MOST 'KEEPERS GUESS WHICH WAY IT'S GOING TO GO - THEN DIVE EITHER LEFT OR RIGHT. DIVING AFTER THE BALL HAS BEEN HIT ONLY GIVES YOU A SMALL CHANCE OF REACTING IN TIME."

5 THE FAKE!
"MOST GOALKEEPERS WILL TRY TO GET THE TAKER TO CHANGE HIS MIND BY FAKING TO DIVE IN A CERTAIN DIRECTION. JUST BEFORE THE STRIKE, THROW YOUR ARMS IN THE OPPOSITE WAY THAT YOU INTEND TO DIVE, THEN GO THE OTHER WAY. IF YOU DO IT PROPERLY, YOU'LL UNSETTLE THE TAKER!"

6 THE DIVE!
"IT'S MUCH HARDER FOR A GOALKEEPER TO GET DOWN TO A LOW SHOT THAN A HIGH ONE. STRIKERS KNOW THIS, SO MOST WILL AIM FOR ONE OF THE BOTTOM CORNERS. THE CHANCES ARE YOU'LL NEED TO DIVE LOW TO ONE OF THE CORNERS IF YOU WANT TO SAVE IT!"

7 THE SAVE!
"IF YOU'VE DIVED THE CORRECT WAY, ALL YOU HAVE TO DO NOW IS MAKE THE SAVE! KEEP YOUR WRISTS LOCKED AND MAKE SURE THAT YOU EITHER PUSH THE BALL AWAY FROM GOAL OR SEND IT OVER THE BAR. SIMPLY BLOCKING THE BALL IS NO GOOD AS IT COULD END UP REBOUNDING BACK TO THE TAKER!"

RAUL · REAL MADRID

WORLD SUPER STRIKERS

GARY NEVILLE'S... TOP TI FOR DEFENDER

Want to be a top international defender? **MATCH** brings you rock-solid defending tips from one of the best in the business – **MAN. UNITED** and **ENGLAND** star **GARY NEVILLE!**

WATCH THE BALL LIKE A HAWK!

GARY SAYS: "Never turn your back on the ball. Keep facing it, even if you have to twist your body to get a good view of it. Always watch the ball and never the opposition player's eyes! Players can use their eyes to try to trick a defender, by looking one way and then going the other way – but the ball doesn't lie!"

TOP TIP
Stand on a line and pass the ball to a mate. Then get them to try to beat you and cross the line. Watch the ball at all times and try to win the ball back off them before they cross the line!

NEVER TURN YOUR BACK ON ATTACKERS!

GARY SAYS: "When a player is about to cross, never turn your back on him. This isn't easy, because it's a natural reaction to try to protect yourself. But if you do, the attacker can dummy you or cut back inside. Never jump in the air or close your eyes – just face the ball straight on. It might hurt if you get hit, but that's your job!"

TOP TIP
Practise stopping a mate from crossing the ball. It doesn't matter if you block it – just focus on keeping your feet on the floor and face the ball. You'll feel more confident and brave in games!

BE POSITIVE WHEN YOU'RE TACKLING!

GARY SAYS: "Being a defender doesn't mean you have to be negative – be positive at all times. It's your job to win the ball, so go and try to win it! Don't stand back and wait for the attacker to beat you. Enjoy winning the ball, because making a good tackle is just as good as scoring a goal! Never pull out and always believe you can win every tackle."

TOP TIP
Mark out a small area, then – using one ball – you and a mate have 60 seconds to tackle each other as many times as you can! The winner is whoever makes the most tackles, so get stuck in!

BE PATIENT AND DON'T DIVE IN!

GARY SAYS: "If a striker is running with the ball and you can't see a chance to win it, don't dive in. You'll either commit a foul or they'll beat you and leave you on the floor! Be patient, because they might knock the ball too far in front of themselves or let it go too close to you. That's your chance to win it!"

TOP TIP
Stand in front of a cone and pass the ball to a mate. He has to hit the cone with the ball and you have to stop him! If you're patient and don't jump in, you'll see how easy it is to defend the cone!

PS S!

HEADING THE BALL TO SAFETY!

GARY SAYS: "When heading the ball out of defence, direction is everything. Get it right and your team is on the attack, but get it wrong and it could leave the opposition with a run at goal! When the ball is in the air, have a quick look around and decide where you want to head it – out of play, to a team-mate or back to the 'keeper."

TOP TIP

Get your mates to form a circle and stand in the middle. Ask one of them to throw the ball in the air, then head it back to another mate. Keep going around the circle before swapping places!

MAKE THE RIGHT CHOICE EVERY TIME!

GARY SAYS: "The difference between a top defender and a poor one is their decision-making, knowing when to tackle and when to stand back. That's all down to concentration. It's the most important aspect of defending, and the players who don't concentrate in training are normally the ones who make mistakes in games."

TOP TIP

Always take training matches as seriously as a game. You'll find yourself in the same situations in training as you do in real matches, so focus in training and you'll instinctively know what to do!

MATCHMAN'S QUIZ!

MY SCORE! /50

ANSWERS ON PAGES 92-93!

GET READY TO BAG A FAT HAT-TRICK, COZ THIS IS DA THIRD OF ME WICKED QUIZZES!

ENGLAND QUIZ!

HOW MUCH DO YA KNOW ABOUT DA MIGHTY ENGLAND FOOTY TEAM? PROVE IT BY SCRIBBLIN' YER ANSWERS IN THE BOXES BELOW!

1 England were drawn in Group B with France, Croatia and which other country at Euro 2004? *ANSWER*

2 Which famous Real Madrid star and free-kick expert is the current captain of England? *ANSWER*

3 In what year did Sven Goran Eriksson become the manager of England? *ANSWER*

4 Which top sports brand makes England's stylish home and away kits? *ANSWER*

5 Which South American country knocked England out of the 2002 World Cup finals? *ANSWER*

6 How many times have England won the European Championships in their history? *ANSWER*

7 Who was the manager of England when they won the World Cup in 1966? *ANSWER*

8 Which country was England's midfield dynamo Owen Hargreaves actually born in? *ANSWER*

9 Against which country did star striker Wayne Rooney score his first ever England goal? *ANSWER*

10 Which qualifying group have England been drawn in for the 2006 World Cup? *ANSWER*

1 POINT FOR EACH CORRECT ANSWER | **MY SCORE** /10

ANDRIY SHEVCHENKO QUIZ!

HOW MUCH DO YA KNOW ABOUT DA LEGENDARY AC MILAN STRIKER? WRITE YOUR ANSWERS HERE!

1 Which country does Shevchenko play his international footy for?

2 Which club did the goal-hungry striker leave to join AC Milan?

3 How much did the Milan hotshot cost – £16 million or £20 million?

4 What squad number does Andriy wear for the Italian giants?

5 In what year did Sheva win the Champions League with AC Milan?

2 POINTS FOR EACH CORRECT ANSWER | **MY SCORE** /10

CHAMPO LEAGUE CHALLENGE!

CIRCLE DA FIVE PLAYERS WHO HAVE LIFTED DA CHAMPIONS LEAGUE TROPHY!

RAUL | VAN NISTELROOY | HARGREAVES | STAM | JUNINHO

OWEN | MALDINI | DECO | OKOCHA | TOTTI

2 POINTS FOR EACH CORRECT ANSWER | **MY SCORE** /10

NATIONAL DRESS!

WHO'S THIS SCOTTISH FOOTY DUDE DRESSED UP IN A CHILLY SCOTTISH KILT?

ANSWER

10 POINTS FOR CORRECT ANSWER | **MY SCORE** /10

KIT MATCH-UP!

WHICH TOP FOOTY BRANDS HAVE MADE THESE ACE PREMIERSHIP KITS THIS SEASON?

1 Arsenal ARSENAL | **2** Liverpool LIVERPOOL | **3** Chelsea CHELSEA | **4** Spurs SPURS | **5** Newcastle NEWCASTLE

A Reebok REEBOK | **B** Umbro UMBRO | **C** adidas ADIDAS | **D** Nike NIKE | **E** Kappa KAPPA

2 POINTS FOR EACH CORRECT ANSWER | **MY SCORE** /10

RONALDO • BRAZIL

WORLD SUPER STRIKERS

WSS

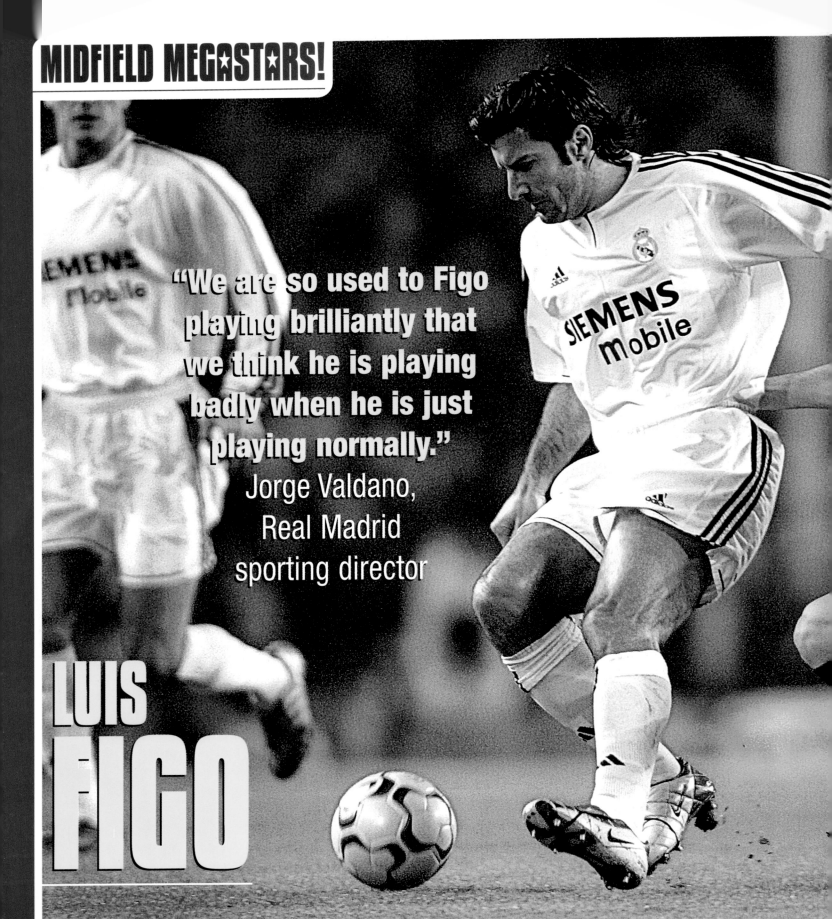

MIDFIELD MEGASTARS!

"We are so used to Figo playing brilliantly that we think he is playing badly when he is just playing normally."
Jorge Valdano,
Real Madrid
sporting director

LUIS FIGO

Figo Timeline...

November
A STAR IS BORN!
Luis Madeira Caeiro Figo is born in Almada, near Portugal's capital, Lisbon.
1972

1984

June
SNAPPED UP!
Joins Sporting Lisbon's junior side after being spotted playing in the street aged 11.

June
EURO WINNER!
Wins his first major honour as Portugal claim the European Under-16 Championship.
1989

October
PRO DEBUT!
Makes his full debut for Sporting Lisbon at the age of just 16.
1991

June
WORLD WINNERS!
Wins World Under-20 Championship on home soil in a Portugal team with Figo, Couto and Rui Costa.

September
PORTU-GEEZER!
Wins his first senior cap aged 18 in the 1-1 friendly draw with Luxembourg.
1992

November
GOAL-DEN BOY!
Scores his first international goal for Portugal in a 2-1 friendly win against Bulgaria.

November
WORLD CUP WOE!
Fails to make the 1994 World Cup finals, after Portugal finish behind Italy and Switzerland in their qualifying group.
1993

May
CUP KINGS!
Wins the Portuguese Cup, and finishes runner-up in the league, in his last season with Sporting.
1995

July
BARÇA BOY!
Replaces Barcelona hero Michael Laudrup at Barcelona in a £1.4 million deal.

MATCH checks out the career of *REAL MADRID*'s *LUIS FIGO*!

Every once in a while, a footballer comes along who completely captures a country's imagination. In Portugal, that player is Luis Figo.

Not since Eusebio set the world alight in the 1960s has one player carried the hopes of the Portuguese public. Luis Figo isn't just another player in the Portugal side, or even just the captain of the team – to many, he is the Portugal team!

Even from a young age, it was clear the midfielder was going to be something special. A European Youth Championship winner at 16 and a World Youth champion at 19, Figo was part of a new breed of Portuguese stars who were called 'The Golden Generation'.

And in a glittering career that's taken him from Sporting Lisbon to Barcelona and on to Real Madrid, it's been success after success. From league titles to Cup Winners' Cups, he's also been a Champions League winner, a World Player Of The Year and won over 100 caps for his country – the 31-year-old star really has won the lot.

Now it's time for MATCH to tell you the amazing story of how Figo became a midfield megastar!

CAREER FACTFILE!	
Born: November 2, 1972 in Almada, Portugal	
Nationality: Portuguese	
Position: Midfielder	
Height: 5ft 11ins	
Weight: 11st 8lbs	
Former clubs: Sporting Lisbon, Barcelona	
Signed: From Barcelona for £37 million on July 24, 2000	
Real Madrid debut: v Valencia, September 9, 2000.	
Real Madrid games/goals: 155 games, 39 goals (September 2000 to May 2004)	
Portugal caps/goals: 107 caps, 31 goals (September 1991 to July 2004)	

June

CZECH IT OUT!
Reaches the quarter-finals of Euro '96, where Portugal are beaten 1-0 by a ten-man Czech Republic.
1996

May

TROPHY TRAIL!
Captains his Barcelona team to glory as they win the Spanish league and cup double.
1998

June

EURO STAR!
Scores a cracker against England, as Portugal reach the semi-finals of Euro 2000 before losing to France.
2000
July

REAL DEAL!
Becomes the world's most expensive player when he joins Real Madrid for £37 million.

December

AWARDS GALORE!
Wins the European Player Of The Year award and comes second in the World Player Of The Year.
2001
December

ON TOP OF THE WORLD!
Pips Beckham and Raul to lift the World Player Of The Year award.

May

JUST CHAMPION!
Wins the Champions League with Real as they beat Bayer Leverkusen 2-1 in Glasgow.
2002
June

WORLD OF PAIN!
Struggles with an ankle injury as Portugal crash out in the first round of the 2002 World Cup.

February

TON UP!
Wins his 100th Portugal cap in the friendly 1-1 draw with England in Faro.
2004

July
EURO WOE!
Comes close to winning Euro 2004 with Portugal, but they lose 1-0 in the final to Greece.

1989

SPORTING CHANCE!

Luis Felipe Madeira Caeiro Figo was born on November 2, 1972 in the working-class district of Almada, in the Portuguese capital of Lisbon. Always football mad, a young Figo used to play every night for the street team Os Pastilhas before, at the age of just 11, he joined the junior side of Portuguese giants Sporting Lisbon. His coach back then was Carlos Queiroz, who would later take charge of the midfielder for the Portuguese national team and Real Madrid. "Even then, Luis was ahead of all the rest," said Queiroz. He was right as well, because at the age of just 16, the coach handed Figo his senior debut for the Sporting Lisbon side!

1991

PORTU-GEEZER!

By 1991, the midfield megastar was a key member of a brilliant Portugal Under-20 team that won the World Youth Championship. He was playing alongside the likes of Rui Costa and Fernando Couto in a group that would later be known as 'The Golden Generation'. Figo had also become a regular in the Sporting Lisbon side, where he wowed the fans with his quick feet and dribbling. This massive talent was getting bigger, and he was becoming impossible to ignore, so it was no real surprise when the 19-year-old was handed his full international debut in a friendly against Luxembourg later that year. If anyone had any doubts before, the message was clear now: Figo had landed and was set to become a huge star!

1995

BARÇA BOUND!

Figo was the captain of Sporting by the age of 22, helping them to glory in the Portuguese Cup and second place in the Portuguese league in 1995. It seemed only a matter of time before Europe's big guns came knocking, and that summer they did – loads of them! Luis was spoilt for choice and signed pre-contract deals with Italian giants Juventus and Parma. This wasn't allowed, so FIFA banned him from moving to an Italian team for two years. With other clubs dithering, Barcelona snapped him up for a bargain £1.4 million!

1997

TRIPLE TROPHY HAUL!

Figo's second season at the Nou Camp saw him pick up his first trophies. As well as winning a Spanish Cup and Super Cup double, the star midfielder was a key figure as the Catalan club lifted the European Cup Winners' Cup. In the final against Paris St Germain, a Ronaldo penalty was enough to give Barcelona victory. And if Figo was thinking about getting a bigger trophy cabinet, he had even more reason to buy one the following season. He was the new captain of a Barça side which stormed La Liga, finishing nine points ahead of nearest rivals Athletic Bilbao. They also lifted the Spanish Cup for the second year running, meaning the Portugal trickster had won five trophies in just two years!

2000

WATCH OUT WORLD!

Portugal went into Euro 2000 as one of the tournament's dark horses, and all eyes were on star man Luis Figo. But at 2-0 down after 18 minutes of their first game against England, things weren't looking good. They needed a hero, and found one in the ace midfielder. He scored a 35-yard screamer to get the score back to 2-1, then ripped the England defence apart as Portugal won 3-2 to cap an amazing comeback. Figo and the Portuguese went from strength to strength – beating Romania and Germany in the group stages, and Turkey in the quarter-finals – before crashing out to a last-gasp extra-time penalty against France in the semis. But the message was clear – Figo wasn't just one of the top players in Europe, he was one of the best in the world. And it wasn't long before Real Madrid, one of the best teams in the world, made him the most expensive player in the world when they signed him for a whopping £37 million!

2000

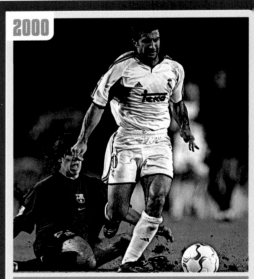

EURO STAR!

Instead of being weighed down by his massive £37 million price tag, Figo went from strength to strength in Madrid. In his first game for Los Galacticos, he scored an 85th-minute winner against Valencia, and won over any fans who still weren't convinced about the player who had moved from their most hated rivals Barcelona. The midfield star's form soon helped Real to the top of the table and that – along with his brilliant showing at Euro 2000 and fantastic form for Barça in the second half of the season – saw Figo receive the worldwide fame his midfield magic deserved. He may have finished runner-up behind Zinedine Zidane in the World Player Of The Year voting, but he scooped the European Player Of The Year award, becoming the first Portuguese star since Eusebio in 1965 to win the title! All of a sudden, the £37 million Real paid for him was looking like a bargain!

2001

WORLD BEATER!

If 2000 had been a good year for Luis Figo, 2001 was even better! The Portuguese star carried on his fine form in the second half of the 2000-01 season, helping Real to their first La Liga title in four years. They also lifted the 2001 Spanish Super Cup and reached the semi-finals of the Champions League. So while it may not have come as a massive shock, it was still a massive honour when Figo picked up the World Player Of The Year award to add to the European honour he'd won 12 months earlier. He left Man. United star David Beckham in second place, and Real Madrid team-mate Raul in third. It was what many people had thought for a long time – Luis Figo was the greatest player on the planet!

2002

JUST CHAMPION!

After crashing out in the semis the previous year, Figo and Real Madrid were desperate to go one better in the 2001-02 Champions League. They went about their mission like they meant business, and the midfielder scored three goals in six group stage games – in both meetings with Roma and the game against Lokomotiv Moscow – as Real topped their group. Los Galacticos charged to the final after beating fierce rivals Barcelona in the semis, but a troublesome ankle injury nearly ruled Figo out of the final against Bayer Leverkusen in Glasgow. The midfielder played through the pain, helping Real to a 2-1 lead before he had to be substituted after an hour. But Madrid managed to hold on, and the Portugal star added yet another medal to his ever-growing collection!

"Luis is technically perfect, quick off the mark and a great dribbler and striker."
Juup Heynkes, former Real Madrid coach

2002

WORLD CUP WOE!

Crowned a champion of Europe with Real a few weeks earlier, Figo should have gone to the World Cup on a high – but Portugal were lucky he was there at all. His ankle injury needed an operation, but Figo played through the pain again to help his country. Many people were expecting big things from Portugal following their run to the semis at Euro 2000, but instead they went out with a whimper. In their first match Portugal lost 3-2 to the USA, before getting back on track by beating Poland 4-0. Everyone thought they'd stroll through to the next stage, but a shock 1-0 defeat to South Korea in the next game sent Figo and Portugal on the first plane home!

2004

EURO 2004 HEARTACHE!

Just a few months after winning his 100th cap for Portugal in a friendly against England, Euro 2004 was massive for Figo in so many ways. The finals were staged in his home country, and – after deciding to retire from international football at the end of the competition – it was the last chance of glory for the Real Madrid midfielder and the rest of the Golden Generation from the 1991 World Youth Championship-winning side. And Portugal came so close! After a shock defeat against Greece in the opening game of the tournament, they beat Russia, Spain, England and Holland to set up an unlikely re-match against the under-rated Greeks in the final. As captain, Figo tried to lead by example with his tricks, flicks and dribbles, but it wasn't enough, and Greece broke Portuguese hearts by winning 1-0 in the Estadio da Luz. Portugal fans were desperate for Luis Figo to change his mind about retiring from the national team, but after a lot of thought, he decided to stick with his decision. Footy will miss you, Luis!

PLANET FOOTY!

LAST 5 WORLD CUP WINNERS!

1986	1990	1994	1998	2002
 Argentina!	 Germany!	 Brazil!	 France!	 Brazil!

THE 2006 WORLD CUP QUALIFIERS!
IN NUMBERS!

The World Cup qualifiers are here, so check out MATCH's 30-second guide to the international footy-fest!

67,000!

Four of England's five home qualifiers will be held at Old Trafford – so 67,000 of you will be able to watch each match at Man. United's wicked stadium!

196!

Across the whole footy-shaped globe, a massive 196 countries will be trying to qualify for the 2006 World Cup!

Only 32 teams will make it to the 2006 World Cup finals in Germany – but as hosts, Germany don't have to qualify!

32!

2,452!

A mammoth 2,452 goals were scored in all the World Cup 2002 qualifiers – so expect a goal-fest!

900!

England will play ten qualifiers – home and away against Wales, N. Ireland, Austria, Poland and Azerbaijan. That's 900 minutes of exciting England footy!

A total of 28 billion people will watch all the World Cup qualifiers on TV!

28 BILLION!

16!

England scored 16 goals to qualify for the 2002 World Cup!

27!

Michael Owen had scored 27 goals for England before the start of the World Cup qualifiers, making him England's leading scorer in the squad!

Including group matches and play-offs, 847 qualifying matches will be played!

847!

40!

By the time the World Cup finals start in June 2006, it will be 40 years since England last lifted the famous trophy!

The last time Germany hosted a World Cup was in 1974 – and England didn't qualify! But Sven's boys will be well up for this one!

1974!

ANDRIY SHEVCHENKO - AC MILAN

ROBBIE KEANE
MY F1RST...

TOTTENHAM and **REPUBLIC OF IRELAND** super striker
ROBBIE KEANE goes back in time with **MATCH!**

MY FIRST MATCH AS A FOOTY FAN!

"I played for a youth team called Crumlin United in Ireland and we watched Man. United play Sheffield Wednesday at Old Trafford when I was 12. Steve Bruce got two headers in the last few minutes!"

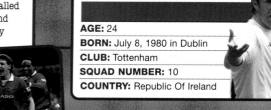

AGE: 24
BORN: July 8, 1980 in Dublin
CLUB: Tottenham
SQUAD NUMBER: 10
COUNTRY: Republic Of Ireland

MY FIRST FOOTY HERO!

"I was a Liverpool fan when I was growing up, so I looked up to players like Ian Rush and John Barnes. I used to watch Ian Rush for his goals and John Barnes for his silky skills. They were both my idols as a boy!"

MY FIRST FOOTBALL KIT!

"I think it was one of those really old-style kits, with the tight shirts and little red shorts that cost about £4! It wasn't anything special! I don't remember any really fashionable kits."

MY FIRST PROFESSIONAL GAME!

"My first pro game was for Wolves against Norwich in 1997. We won 2-0 and I scored two goals, so it was an incredible debut! It was fantastic to be playing for a top team and my family were at the game too, so to score two goals was even better for me!"

MY FIRST GAME FOR SPURS!

"My first game for Spurs was in 2002 against West Ham. It was good to start off at home and in a London derby – the atmosphere was tremendous. You always remember your first game because the fans really welcome you!"

MY FIRST GOAL FOR SPURS!

"It was against Blackburn away, but I had to wait a bit! I didn't score for about three or four games after joining Spurs, so it was a bit of a relief when the first goal came!"

MY FIRST HAT-TRICK!

"My first hat-trick was against Everton in January 2003 when we won 4-3, and I scored all three goals in the second half. That game was the last time my dad saw me play before he passed away, so it was a special match for me."

MY FIRST CAR!

"My first car was a Fiat Bravo, but I've treated myself to a few now! I've got a Range Rover and it's nice because it's really comfortable!"

MY FIRST GAME FOR IRELAND!

"I played against the Czech Republic for 20 minutes and then I made my full debut against Argentina at home. We lost but I was Man Of The Match! I then scored two goals against Malta, so I was pleased with the start I made for Ireland."

MY FIRST WORLD CUP!

"It was great to play for Ireland in the 2002 World Cup! As a kid, you dream of playing in a World Cup, so to be there was great, and to score a few goals was something special for me. There's no other feeling like it in football."

MATCHMAN'S QUIZ!

YOU MIGHT 'AVE DONE OKAY SO FAR, BUT LET'S SEE HOW YA GET ON WITH ME FOURTH QUIZ!

HEAD SPIN!

ME EYES 'AVE GONE ALL GOGGLY! CAN YA TELL WHO THIS TOP FOOTY PLAYER IS?

10 POINTS FOR CORRECT ANSWER

MY SCORE /10

1. I was born on March 2, 1982 in Rio de Janeiro, Brazil.

2. I am a top striker who played for Germany in Euro 2004.

3. I play my club footy for VfB Stuttgart in the Bundesliga.

4. I scored against Man. United in the Champions League clash in Stuttgart last season.

5. I scored four goals in 14 games for my country before drawing a blank at Euro 2004.

ANSWER

BARCELONA QUIZ!

HOW MUCH DO YA KNOW ABOUT THE SPANISH GIANTS? WRITE YOUR ANSWERS IN THE BOXES BELOW!

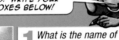

1 What is the name of Barcelona's massive footy stadium?

2 How many European Cups have the Catalan giants won in their history?

3 In what position did Barcelona finish in the La Liga table last season?

4 What is the name of the current coach (pictured left) of Barça?

5 True or false – England hero Gary Lineker used to play for Barcelona?

2 POINTS FOR EACH CORRECT ANSWER

MY SCORE /10

SPOT THE DIFFERENCE!

CAN YA FIND DA FIVE DIFFERENCES BETWEEN THESE TWO PICS? CIRCLE 'EM ALL!

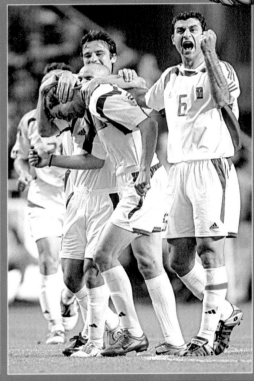

2 POINTS FOR EACH CORRECT ANSWER

MY SCORE /10

CAP in hand!

HOW MANY CAPS DID GEORDIE HITMAN ALAN SHEARER BAG FOR ENGLAND?

a) 54

b) 63

c) 72

ANSWER

10 POINTS FOR CORRECT ANSWER

MY SCORE /10

PASTA OR PAELLA?

ANTONIO CASSANO	ALBERTO LUQUE	DAVID ALBELDA	ANDREA PIRLO	MASSIMO ODDO
ANSWER	ANSWER	ANSWER	ANSWER	ANSWER

WHICH STARS PLAY FOR ITALY AND WHICH PLAY FOR SPAIN? SCRIBBLE 'PASTA' NEXT TO THE ITALIANS AND 'PAELLA' UNDER THE SPANIARDS!

2 POINTS FOR EACH CORRECT ANSWER

MY SCORE /10

MICHAEL OWEN · ENGLAND

WORLD SUPER STRIKERS

GERRARD: MY

Born in Whiston hospital in 1980, Steven Gerrard joined the youth academy at Liverpool Football Club in 1988 and has never looked back.

After starring in the youth and reserve teams at Anfield, he was handed his Liverpool debut by Gerard Houllier in the 1998-99 season. He became a massive star and in May 2000, the call came from England manager Kevin Keegan.

Since then, Gerrard has scored amazing goals, won stacks of trophies and played in some of the most memorable games in recent footy history – including England's 5-1 thrashing of rivals Germany!

So how did an ordinary kid from Liverpool become one of the most admired – and most wanted – players in world football? MATCH opened Steven Gerrard's brilliant career scrapbook to find out!

▲ LIVERPOOL THROUGH AND THROUGH!

Steven Gerrard has been a Liverpool fan all his life, and now he's living a dream as the captain of the club he supported as a boy. After signing a new contract in November 2003, he said: **"I've been here since I was eight years old and there's never been a single moment when I've wanted to play for someone else."** But a big-money offer from Chelsea at the end of the season made Gerrard think hard about his future. His love of Liverpool persuaded him to stay though, and now he's determined to bring silverware back to Anfield!

SCRAPBOOK!

◄ STEVIE G'S DEBUT! ►

Steven made his Liverpool debut in the 2-0 win over Blackburn in 1998 (left). He played in his first Merseyside derby a year later in a 3-2 win, and scored his first goal against Everton in 2001 – a 3-1 victory at Goodison!

▲ ENGLAND CALL-UP! ►

After impressing for Liverpool, Kevin Keegan invited him to train with the England squad, where team-mate Robbie Fowler and ex-Red Steve McManaman helped him settle in.

England manager Kevin Keegan presents Stevie with his first international cap ahead of his debut against the Ukraine.

◄ ENGLAND DEBUT!

After injury ruled Gerrard out of the squad to play Argentina in February 2000, he made his long-awaited England debut against the Ukraine at Wembley on May 31, 2000. He got off to a winning start thanks to goals from Robbie Fowler (below) and Tony Adams. It was a mature performance from the 19-year-old Liverpool midfielder, who celebrated his 20th birthday the day after the 2-0 victory!

◄ WORTHY CUP WINNER! ►

Stevie won his first trophy in the 2001 Worthington Cup final against Birmingham. Liverpool took the lead through Robbie Fowler's 25-yard lob, but City equalised in stoppage time and the game went to penalties. Gerrard was substituted 14 minutes from time due to injury, but he cheered on his team-mates from the sidelines, then ran on to celebrate as Birmingham missed their last penalty!

GERRARD'S big moments!

MAY 1980

Born in Whiston on May 30, 1980. Watched his first game at Anfield aged five, and joined the club's academy aged eight.

NOVEMBER 1998

Made his debut for Liverpool aged 18, as an 89th-minute substitute against Blackburn on November 29, 1998. His full debut came six days later, and he was named Man Of The Match in his third game against Celta Vigo in the UEFA Cup.

APRIL 1999

Played in his first Merseyside derby on April 3, 1999. He cleared Danny Cadamarteri's shot off the line to hand The Reds a 3-2 win over Everton.

SEPTEMBER 1999

Sent off at Anfield in the 161st Merseyside derby after a lunge at Kevin Campbell, with rivals Everton finishing 1-0 winners.

NOVEMBER 1999

Made his debut for England's Under-21 side in a 5-0 win over Luxembourg and scored the first goal! Gerrard made three more appearances for the Under-21s, against Poland, Denmark and Yugoslavia.

DECEMBER 1999

Scored his first Liverpool goal in a 4-1 win against Sheffield Wednesday. Picking up the ball 30 yards out, the 19-year-old charged forward from midfield, took on two defenders and slid the ball past the 'keeper!

FEBRUARY 2000

Called up to the full England squad by Kevin Keegan for the friendly against Argentina, but an injury forced the Liverpool ace to pull out of the squad.

◄▲ 30-YARD SCREAMER!

Playing against Man. United brings out the best in Steven Gerrard. In March 2001, he struck a sensational 30-yard drive that swung and dipped in the air before crashing into the net past a stunned Fabien Barthez. The goal helped Liverpool to a 2-0 win at Anfield, and in 2004 it was voted the club's best ever Premiership goal!

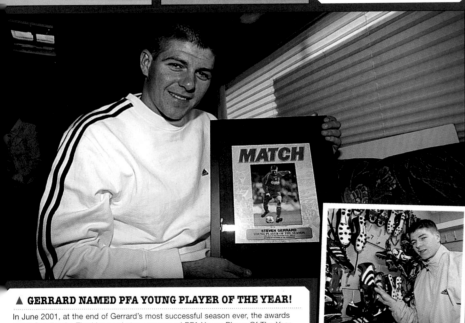

"Fancy cleaning these for me, MATCH?" Stevie G in the famous Anfield boot room with his flash Adidas Predator boots!

▲ GERRARD NAMED PFA YOUNG PLAYER OF THE YEAR!

In June 2001, at the end of Gerrard's most successful season ever, the awards came flooding in. The Liverpool star was named PFA Young Player Of The Year by his fellow pros, while MATCH readers named him 2001 Young Gun Of The Year in our Readers Poll, with a huge 64 per cent of the votes. A thrilled Gerrard said: "I'm delighted to win this award – it's great! I'm a bit surprised, because there are a lot of very good young players around at the moment, so for me to get 64 per cent of the vote is fantastic. I must be doing something right!"

◄ FA CUP WINNER! ►

Just three months after winning the Worthington Cup, Gerrard was back in Cardiff as Liverpool faced Arsenal in the 2001 FA Cup final. They went 1-0 down with Freddie Ljungberg's 77th-minute goal, and The Gunners were on top – but Stevie G and his team-mates kept battling, and they equalised in the 83rd minute thanks to Michael Owen. Then, with two minutes left, Owen scored a fantastic winner, outpacing the Arsenal back four to score past David Seaman!

◀ UEFA CUP WINNER! ▶

Gerrard's 2000-01 season ended in a nine-goal UEFA Cup final! Liverpool took the lead after just three minutes, before Stevie G put The Reds 2-0 up with a great finish. Alaves came back into it, and at the end of a thrilling 90 minutes it was 4-4! An own goal won it for Liverpool, handing Steven his third trophy of an incredible season!

Stevie G celebrates with his team-mates after Robbie Fowler scores in Liverpool's 5-4 win over Alaves in the UEFA Cup final!

GERRARD'S big moments!

MAY 2000

Promoted from the Under-21s, Gerrard made his full England debut against the Ukraine in a 2-0 victory at Wembley.

JUNE 2000

Selected in the England squad for Euro 2000. Played in a 1-0 win over Germany, but injured for the 3-2 defeat to Romania which sent England home.

DECEMBER 2000

Named Man Of The Match in Liverpool's 4-0 thrashing of Arsenal at Anfield, scoring the first goal with a powerful drive.

MARCH 2001

Lifted his first trophy in the 2001 League Cup final when Liverpool beat Birmingham City in a penalty shoot-out at the Millennium Stadium.

MARCH 2001

Scored a 30-yard screamer against rivals Man. United in a 2-0 victory at Anfield. In 2004, it was voted Liverpool's best Premiership goal ever.

MAY 2001

Picked up his second trophy of the 2000-01 season by beating Arsenal 2-1 in the FA Cup final at the Millennium Stadium.

MAY 2001

Collected his third trophy of the season in the 5-4 UEFA Cup victory over Alaves. Scored the second goal in Liverpool's first European triumph in 17 years.

MAY 2001

Voted PFA Young Player Of The Year by his fellow pros, and named Young Gun Of The Year in the MATCH Readers Poll.

SEPTEMBER 2001

Turned the World Cup qualifier against Germany on its head by scoring a wonder goal from outside the area with the score at 1-1. Sven Goran Eriksson's side went on to win 5-1.

GERRARD IN GOAL? ▶

We knew Steven Gerrard played at right-back in his first few matches for Liverpool, but we didn't know he was a goalkeeper until we saw him in a penalty shoot-out for Powerade!

◀ GERMANY THRASHED!

After a poor start to their World Cup qualifying campaign, England badly needed a victory against Germany in September 2001. The Germans took an early lead, but Michael Owen equalised and Gerrard blasted his country in front with a stunning drive from outside the area. England were on fire, and Stevie set up Owen for his hat-trick as England won 5-1!

▲ 2002 WORLD CUP AGONY!

Stevie was dealt the biggest blow of his career when he was ruled out of the 2002 World Cup in South Korea & Japan. He suffered a groin injury in the last game of the 2001-02 season against Ipswich, which needed an operation before he could play again. It was hard to take for the young Liverpool star, especially after he had overcome the growing pains that had affected the start of his career.

Stevie poses for MATCH while taking a well-earned rest from charging up and down the pitch for Liverpool and England!

▲ LIVERPOOL CAPTAIN!

In October 2003, Steven Gerrard was named as the new captain of Liverpool, starting in the UEFA Cup match against Olimpija Ljubljana. **"It was a bit of a shock when the manager told me,"** said Gerrard at the time. **"But I have been made captain of one of the biggest clubs in Europe and I'm really proud!"**

Taking a break from shooting a TV advert for Adidas, where he was filmed playing a game of street footy with some kids!

◄ ENGLAND CAPTAIN!

One of the best moments of Steven's career was being made captain for England's game against Sweden in the build-up to Euro 2004. And Gerrard had mixed emotions as England lost 1-0. **"It was strange – I was disappointed with the score, but at the same time I was very proud to captain my country."**

AMAZING FINAL GOAL! ▶

The Millennium Stadium had become a lucky ground for Liverpool. In 2003, they reached the Worthington Cup final and faced rivals Man. United. Stevie G opened the scoring after 39 minutes with an amazing 30-yard drive, goalkeeper Jerzy Dudek kept Liverpool in the game with some awesome saves, and Michael Owen made sure The Reds lifted the trophy with a goal four minutes from time!

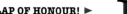

▲ LAP OF HONOUR! ▶

At the end of the 2003-04 season, Liverpool were involved in a fight for the Premiership's final Champions League place. They did it with wins against Man. United, Middlesbrough and Birmingham, and to celebrate – on the last day of the season against Newcastle – Stevie took his daughter Lily Ella on a lap of the Anfield pitch!

▲ JONNY AND STEVIE!

Two of the biggest names in English sport came together to promote the new Adidas Predator boot ready for Euro 2004. Jonny Wilkinson chose rugby over football at a very young age – even though his grandfather had been a professional footy star for Norwich City. Thankfully, Stevie has always been a football man!

Stevie G's fiancée, Alex Curran, watches him playing for England!

HITTING THE HEIGHTS WITH ENGLAND AT EURO 2004! ▲

England went to Euro 2004 with high hopes. And after missing the 2002 World Cup, Gerrard was desperate to impress for his country, starting with the opening match against holders France! But after taking the lead through a Frank Lampard header, Zinedine Zidane struck twice in injury-time to give France a 2-1 win.

England roared back in their second game against Switzerland, with Gerrard scoring after a fine passing move in a 3-0 win. Their good form continued in the final group game, where Stevie G was at his best in a brilliant 4-2 victory over Croatia. But a quarter-final defeat to Portugal meant Gerrard would have to wait until the 2006 World Cup for another chance to lift a trophy with England!

Stevie G has comforting words for England team-mate Darius Vassell!

GERRARD'S
big moments!

MARCH 2002

Helped Liverpool to the quarter-finals of the Champions League with a 2-0 victory over Roma. The win was dedicated to Reds manager Gerard Houllier on his return from heart surgery.

MAY 2002

Guided Liverpool to second spot in the league behind Arsenal. But a groin injury in the last game of the season ruled him out of the 2002 World Cup.

OCTOBER 2002

Lost possession in a Euro 2004 qualifier, handing a 2-1 lead to opponents Macedonia. But he scored the equaliser by chesting the ball in the air and crashing home a brilliant 20-yard volley.

MARCH 2003

Lifted the Worthington Cup for the second time after scoring against Man. United in a 2-0 win at the Millennium Stadium. Scored twice in the Premiership to be named Barclaycard Player Of The Month for March.

JUNE 2003

Scored a cracking goal against Serbia & Montenegro. Starting the move on the halfway line, he played a one-two with Frank Lampard, passed to Michael Owen, then raced into the box to fire home the return ball!

OCTOBER 2003

Handed the Liverpool captaincy on a permanent basis ahead of the club's UEFA Cup match against Olimpija Ljubljana.

MARCH 2004

Made England captain by Sven Goran Eriksson for the friendly against Sweden – with David Beckham and Michael Owen unavailable – as the national team prepared for Euro 2004.

MAY 2004

Played an inspirational role as Liverpool finished fourth in the Premiership and gained a Champions League qualifying spot. Gerrard was named in the Premiership Team Of The Year.

JUNE 2004

Impressed in England's group games in Euro 2004, but was substituted in the quarter-final against Portugal with England 1-0 up. The hosts levelled two minutes later, and went on to win the game on penalties.

FOOTY DOGS!

THE ROTTWEILER!
Roy Keane

THE POODLE!
Robert Pires

THE JACK RUSSELL!
Deco

THE BULLDOG!
Wayne Rooney

THE GREYHOUND!
Henrik Larsson

mystic matchman!

MATCHY gazes into his footy-shaped crystal ball to find out what's gonna happen in the future!

August 2005!

Last season's European champions Chelsea are in financial ruin after Roman Abramovich leaves to take over Norwich City. As the Russian billionaire explains: "Yellow is a nicer colour than blue". Aston Villa and Birmingham merge to form a massive club called Birmingham United, as Charlton and Spurs set the early pace in the Premiership.

September 2005!

New Real Madrid boss Arsene Wenger brings Thierry Henry, Robert Pires and Freddie Ljungberg to the Bernabeu. Cristiano Ronaldo quits football to become a ballerina after falling out with Man. United manager Roy Keane. Newcastle boss Alan Shearer snaps up James Beattie for £8 million, and Chelsea release nine players to ease their debts.

October 2005!

Ronaldo signs for Roman Abramovich's Norwich City. Hard-up Leeds are in big trouble after new manager Claudio Ranieri signs Andriy Shevchenko for £72 million without telling anyone. England beat Poland 10-0 and qualify for the 2006 World Cup thanks to five goals each from new strike force Wayne Rooney and Jermain Defoe.

November 2005!

Kevin Keegan makes a shock playing comeback for Man. City and nets a hat-trick against Premiership new boys Gillingham, sparking a new craze of curly black mop-cuts in the blue half of Manchester. Torquay striker Emile Heskey enters the Big Brother house, but is voted out within half an hour, after one of his stray shots kills a chicken.

December 2005!

Christian Vieri and Steven Gerrard join Ronaldo at Norwich. Everton move into their new home stadium in China and field football's first ever robot player up front. Despite being reduced to tears by Simon Cowell in his audition, 2006 Pop Idol winner Wayne Rooney tops the Christmas charts with his debut song – a duet with Charlie from Busted.

January 2006!

Leeds' dodgy financial situation gets even worse after Claudio Ranieri uses too many sheets of bog roll, leaving the club bankrupt. Man. City striker Robbie Fowler is fined £45,000 after reporting back from the Christmas break nearly 12 stone overweight. Blackburn boss Graeme Souness is forced to play physio Dave Fevre after falling out with 23 members of his playing squad.

February 2006!

Man. United launch their new satellite scouting network on Mars – in search of the next generation of inter-galactic talent. Abramovich strikes again as Alessandro Nesta and Carlos Puyol move to Norwich and receive free, gold-plated tractors. Chelsea release another 12 players to cut costs and sign Dion Dublin on a free transfer.

March 2006!

Iain Dowie makes a guest appearance in Harry Potter 4 as a flute-playing ogre. Leeds sell Elland Road on e-bay for £49.99 to a mysterious Mr. A. Ferguson, who turns it into a huge haggis factory. Middlesbrough win the Carling Cup for the third year in a row, and Fulham are knocked out of the Champions League quarter-finals by Roma.

April 2006!

Brazil star Ronaldinho quits football to become a dentist and part-time model. After missing his tenth international penalty of the season, David Beckham is hounded by the press and decides to play for Argentina. The title race between Charlton and Spurs hots up, with both teams level on points.

May 2006!

Charlton Athletic clinch the Premiership title, with the penniless Chelsea finishing bottom of the table, having gained just a single point all season. Ipswich Town win the 2006 FA Cup on penalties. England beat Brazil 5-0 in the opening match at the flash new Wembley Stadium, and Rooney and the boys fly off to Germany as 2-1 favourites to lift the World Cup!

DAVID TREZEGUET · JUVENTUS

MY PROUDEST

GARETH SOUTHGATE
Middlesbrough

"Playing for my country, and just being involved with England for the first time – it's the best thing you can do and the biggest honour to achieve. I was 25 when I got my first call-up and it was very special – my dad and grandad are really proud to be English and I was brought up to be the same!"

PETER WHITTINGHAM
Aston Villa

"When I won the Youth Cup with Aston Villa. We beat Everton in the final and they had Wayne Rooney in their team, so it was great to win! There were a few scares in the early rounds, but it was great to go all the way."

ROBERT PIRES
Arsenal

"For me, my proudest moment was lifting the World Cup with France in 1998 and kissing the trophy! That's the biggest moment you can have in your career."

EDWIN VAN DER SAR
Fulham

"My proudest moment has to be when I won the European Cup with Ajax in 1995. We beat AC Milan twice in the group stages and then we met them again in the final, and it was a great achievement to beat them three times in one tournament! It was the best team I've played in and it was a young team, too. The year after that we started to lose players one at a time. If we'd stayed together a little longer we might have won more."

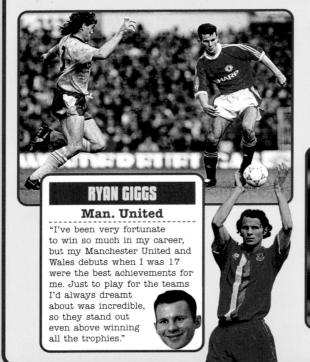

RYAN GIGGS
Man. United

"I've been very fortunate to win so much in my career, but my Manchester United and Wales debuts when I was 17 were the best achievements for me. Just to play for the teams I'd always dreamt about was incredible, so they stand out even above winning all the trophies."

MICHAEL CARRICK
Tottenham

"Playing for England! Making my England debut was probably my proudest moment so far, but then there's reaching the Youth Cup final with West Ham and my first-team debut for West Ham against Newcastle!"

MOMENT!

WAYNE ROONEY
Man. United

"Scoring my first England goal! We were losing 1-0 against Macedonia and it was just after half-time. I remember the ball dropped to me and I hit it as hard as I could and it went into the bottom corner. I think that's been the best moment for me so far. I couldn't believe it when it went in, and I didn't even know where I was running off to afterwards to celebrate!"

MATT UPSON
Birmingham

"Playing for England, because it's every player's dream to represent his country and I'm no different. I was surprised the first time I was called up, but it was very positive for me – an experience I'll always remember. It's really special pulling on the England shirt and singing the national anthem!"

ROBBIE KEANE
Tottenham

"My proudest moment was scoring for Ireland against Germany in the 2002 World Cup. To be playing and scoring in a World Cup for my country was incredible, but to get one in the last minute against Germany in such an important game was just unbelievable!"

JAMIE CARRAGHER
Liverpool

"I'd have to say making my full debut for Liverpool against Aston Villa as an 18-year-old is my proudest moment. Well, that and being named Liverpool captain for the first time – that was a very special moment!"

DIS IS YER LAST CHANCE TO BAG SOME POINTS AND PROVE YOU'RE A FOOTY NUT. GOOD LUCK!

SPOT THE SPIES!

CIRCLE DA FIVE TOP GAFFERS HIDING IN DIS CRAZY CROWD!

2 POINTS FOR EACH CORRECT ANSWER

MY SCORE /10

dream team!

USE THESE CHEEKY LITTLE CLUES TO REVEAL MY FLASH PREMIERSHIP DREAM TEAM! THEN WRITE YER ANSWERS ON DA TEAMSHEET BELOW!

England's young Canary!

GK

ANSWER

Top Welsh Villan!	Fulham's giant youngster!	South African Addick!	Ex-Hearts star at Everton!
RB	CB	CB	LB
Mark Delaney	ANSWER	ANSWER	ANSWER

Stylish Swede at Highbury!	Man. United & Cameroon hardman!	Birmingham & Turkey ace!	Aussie winger at Anfield!
RM	CM	CM	LM
ANSWER	ANSWER	ANSWER	ANSWER

Saints and England hitman! **Newcastle and Wales speedster!**

S   S

ANSWER   ANSWER

1 POINT FOR EACH CORRECT ANSWER

MY SCORE /10

SPORTS MAD!

WHICH FOOTY STAR HAS BEEN DRESSED UP AS A BALL-SMACKIN' TENNIS PLAYER?

ANSWER

10 POINTS FOR CORRECT ANSWER

MY SCORE /10

TROPHY TRACKER!

SEE IF YA CAN SPOT DA TWO TEAMS THAT ARE MISSIN' FROM DIS LIST OF PAST CHAMPIONS LEAGUE WINNERS!

2000	**Real Madrid**	
? 2001 ?	ANSWER	?
? 2002 ?	ANSWER	?
2003	**AC Milan**	
2004	**Porto**	

5 POINTS FOR EACH CORRECT ANSWER

MY SCORE /10

WHAT'S YOUR JOB?

CAN YA MATCH THESE DUDES WITH THEIR JOBS IN FOOTY? SCRIBBLE A LINE BETWEEN THE ONES THAT MATCH!

2 POINTS FOR EACH CORRECT ANSWER

MY SCORE /10

1 ROBBIE EARLE	2 GARY MEGSON	3 MARTIN TYLER	4 DANIEL LEVY	5 ANDERS FRISK
A COMMENTATOR	B CHAIRMAN	C REFEREE	D BLAH! BLAH! BLAH! BLAH! BLAH! PUNDIT	E MANAGER

WORLD SUPER STRIKERS

FERNANDO TORRES · SPAIN

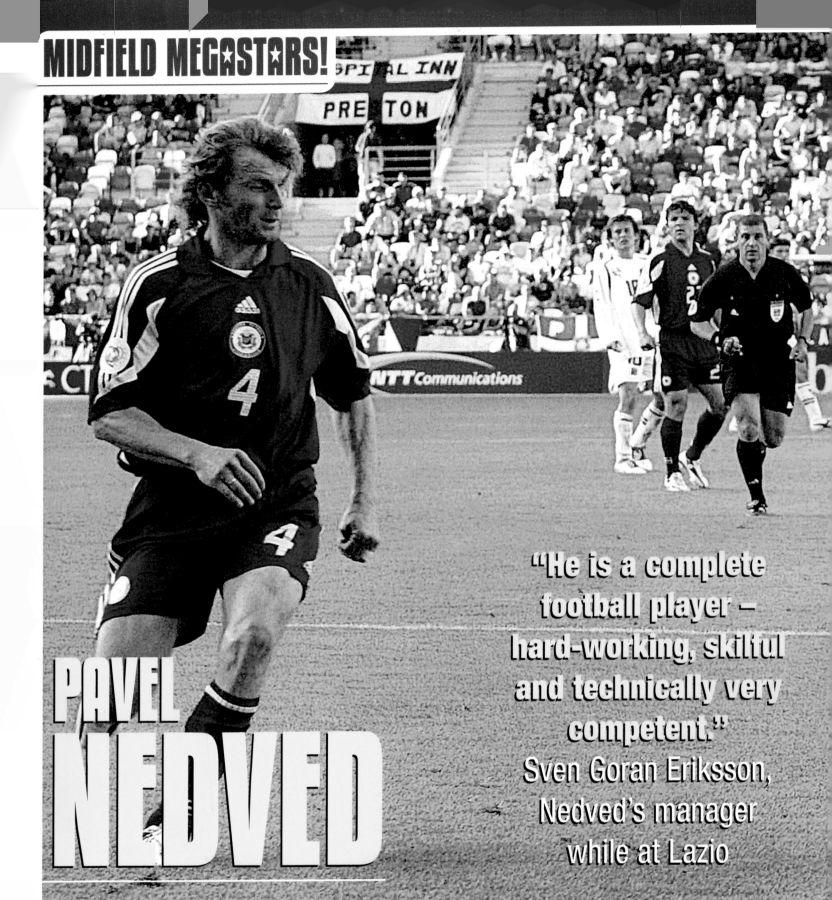

MIDFIELD MEGASTARS!

PAVEL NEDVED

"He is a complete football player – hard-working, skilful and technically very competent."
Sven Goran Eriksson, Nedved's manager while at Lazio

Nedved Timeline...

May 1990 — STARTING OUT!
Pavel's first big club is Skoda Pilsen, who play in the Czechoslovakian Second Division.

May 1992 — DUKLA DEAL!
Moves to top-flight side Dukla Prague and scores three goals in 19 games in his first season with Dukla.

June — BIG BREAK!
Seals a transfer to Sparta Prague, the country's top club, after impressing across town with Dukla.

May 1993 — TROPHY HUNT!
Wins Czech league and cup double in his first season with Sparta Prague.

May 1994 — MORE PRIZES!
Wins second Czech title with Sparta and gets his first taste of Champions League footy.

June — CZECH IN!
Makes his international debut in a 3-1 win over the Republic Of Ireland.

May 1995 — TRIPLE JOY!
It's three in a row for Pavel and Sparta Prague, as they win the title again!

June 1996 — CZECH GOAL!
Scores his first international goal in a 2-1 win over Italy at Euro '96.
FINAL FALL!
Loses to Germany in the final of Euro '96, but Nedved and co. have a fantastic tournament.

July — LAZIO LAND HIM!
Earns a transfer to Italian giants Lazio for £500,000.

May 1998 — COPPA THIS!
Wins the Coppa Italia and the Italian Supercup with Lazio, and is named Czech Player Of The Year. Loses UEFA Cup final to Inter Milan.

MATCH *looks at the career of* **JUVENTUS** *star* **PAVEL NEDVED**!

With his blond mop hair, staring eyes and pointy nose, Pavel Nedved is one of world football's most recognisible figures. But it's his pure football ability on the pitch that really makes him stand out!

Nedved's talent was first spotted in the Czech lower leagues, before he moved to Sparta Prague and claimed three league titles. He hit the big time at Euro '96, where a brilliant Czech Republic team finished runners-up in the final, and Lazio swooped to sign him.

His style is well suited to Italy's Serie A, and he's already won every major domestic honour in Italy, including three league titles. He was adored by the Lazio fans, but he broke their hearts with a £25 million move to Italian rivals Juventus. Pavel has continued to improve his game at Juve though, maturing into a midfield megastar with superb vision, passing, pace and a deadly shot with both feet.

After watching his magical talent at Euro 2004 – where he captained his Czech side to the semi-finals – it's time for MATCH to take an even closer look at his amazing career!

CAREER FACTFILE!

Born: August 30, 1972 in Cheb, Czechoslovakia

Nationality: Czech

Position: Midfielder

Height: 5ft 10ins

Weight: 11st 6lb

Former clubs: Skoda Pilsen, Dukla Prague, Sparta Prague, Lazio

Signed: From Lazio for £25 million on July 12, 2001

Juventus debut: v Venezia, August 26 2001

Juventus games/goals: 125 games, 26 goals (August 2001 to May 2004)

Czech Republic caps/goals: 83 caps, 17 goals (June 1994 to July 2004)

May
CUP KING!
Impresses in Europe with Lazio and scores the winner in the European Cup Winners' Cup final against Real Mallorca.

1999

May
DOUBLE DELIGHT!
It's double delight as he leads Lazio to the league and cup double. He is also named Czech Player Of The Year again!

June
EURO LOSER!
Disappoints for Czech Republic at Euro 2000 as they crash out in the group stages.

2000

July
JUVE JOY!
Signs for Juventus in a £25 million move to replace Zinedine Zidane.

November
RED CARD TROUBLE!
Fails to reach the World Cup finals with the Czech Republic and is sent off in a play-off against Belgium.

2001

May
TITLE PARTY!
Wins the Serie A title with Juventus after scoring four goals in 32 league games.

May

2002

May
MILAN MISERY!
Leads Juventus to the Champions League final, but is suspended as AC Milan lift the trophy.

October
CZECH LEADER!
Steers the Czech Republic to the Euro 2004 finals as team captain, remaining unbeaten in eight qualifiers.

2003

December
EURO STAR!
Picks up the European Player Of The Year award after an awesome year with Juventus and the Czechs.

January
CHELSEA LINK!
He's linked with Chelsea in a £25 million move, but stays as Juve finish third in the league.

2004

July
EURO PAIN!
Storms to the Euro 2004 semi-finals with the Czechs, but there's a shock as he goes off injured and they lose to Greece.

1992

PRAGUE PARTY!

Pavel Nedved was born in Cheb, near Prague, on August 30, 1972. As a kid he was really into sports and his talent with a football was clear to see. Pavel's first big club was Skoda Pilsen, who were in the Czechoslovakian Second Division. He then moved to Dukla Prague, where he scored three goals in 19 games in the 1991-92 season. In 1992, Pavel moved to the country's biggest club, Sparta Prague, and it was there that his career really took off. He played in all sorts of positions, from wing-back to central midfield, and helped Sparta to win three league titles in 1993, 1994 and 1995. The 1995-96 season was his best yet, as he scored 14 goals from midfield as Sparta went on to lift the Czech Cup!

1996

EURO BOY!

Nedved made his international debut for the Czech Republic in 1994, at the age of 21, in a 3-1 win over the Republic Of Ireland, and he was a regular in the side ahead of the Euro '96 championships in England. Drawn in Group C, Nedved and co. lost 2-0 to Germany in their opening match but then beat Italy 2-1 in a game where Pavel scored his first international goal! A 3-3 draw with Russia was enough to see them reach the quarter-finals to face Portugal. Pavel was suspended, but his team still won 1-0 and he returned for the semi-final with France. That game went to penalties, and Pavel converted his crucial spot-kick as the Czechs won 6-5 in sudden death! In the final against Germany – the biggest game of the young midfielder's life – Nedved played well, but the Czech Republic lost by a Golden Goal scored by Oliver Bierhoff. It was a cruel way to lose, but now the whole of Europe knew about his magical talent!

"He is our leader. When you see Pavel Nedved in your team, you are always happy!"
Milan Baros,
Czech Republic

1996

LAZIO COME CALLING!

After his brilliant displays at Euro 96, the all-action Nedved moved to Italian giants Lazio for a bargain fee of around £500,000. Lazio's Czech coach Zdenek Zeman knew he'd signed one of Europe's most talented players, and the midfielder – who was playing on the left wing then – brought pace, vision, goals and energy to the Rome side. The Lazio fans loved their new star and his ability to dribble, pass and shoot with both feet. In his first season, Pavel scored seven Serie A goals and helped the club to finish fourth in the league. The Italian press nicknamed him the 'Furia Ceca', which translated means the Czech Wizard!

1999

CUP HERO!

In 1999, the Czech Wizard won his first major trophy with Lazio by lifting the European Cup Winners' Cup. The season before, he'd helped the Rome outfit to win the Coppa Italia – Italy's FA Cup. But this was Lazio's first European trophy, and it was extra special because they had just lost the title to AC Milan by a single point, and lost the 1998 UEFA Cup final. The Czech star scored three goals for his side, managed by Sven Goran Eriksson, on the way to the Euro final – and he was in superb form before the big night against Real Mallorca. Christian Vieri gave Lazio the lead before Mallorca levelled, but Nedved struck in the 81st minute to win it for the Italians! It was the perfect end to a spectacular season for Pavel – but things were about to get even better!

2000

DOUBLE DELIGHT!

The last time Lazio won the Serie A title was back in 1974, and the fans were desperate to land Italy's biggest prize again. The club's long wait came to an end in 2000 – and they also won the Coppa Italia to make it a brilliant double-winning season. Nedved was the driving force in the team – along with Juan Veron, Alessandro Nesta and Alen Boksic. In fact, he was now considered one of the best all-round midfielders in Europe – quick and skilful yet tough-tackling and energetic. He chipped in with five league goals that season and often played in a free role, creating havoc for the opposition. After four years with the club, Nedved had finally helped Lazio to bring the league trophy home!

2001

JUVENTUS SWOOP!

It was the news Lazio fans didn't want to hear – Nedved was leaving! Following five great years at the Olympic Stadium, including 51 goals in 207 games and seven trophies, Lazio sold their star midfielder to Juventus for £25 million! The pressure was immediately on the Czech Wizard at Juve, because not only did he cost a huge stack of cash, but he was replacing Zinedine Zidane – who had been sold to Real Madrid. Although Nedved was a different type of player to Zidane, he was still expected to fill his role in the Juventus side by scoring goals, creating chances and leading the team. His career in Italy had been a huge success up to that point, but would it stay that way?

2002

THE GOOD AND THE BAD!

Pavel didn't take long to show his class at new club Juventus. His breathtaking performances soon had the fans saying he was even better than Zidane – because his versatility and amazing work-rate were qualities that the Frenchman never showed in Turin. And after another top season, in which he scored four league goals, Juve were crowned Serie A champions. But that success was in contrast to what happened with the Czech Republic. Nedved's country failed to qualify for the 2002 World Cup finals, after losing both legs of their qualifying play-off against Belgium. And to make matters worse, Pavel was sent off in the second leg! Then aged 29, he thought seriously about retiring from the international game!

2003

EUROPE'S BEST!

Following the disappointment of not playing at the World Cup, 'Pocket Rocket' Nedved decided against quitting international footy and buckled down to produce the best form of his career. In 2003 he was awesome for club and country, and was named the European Player Of The Year in December ahead of Zidane, Henry and Ronaldo. The award was well deserved – he captained a Czech side that qualified for Euro 2004 without losing, steered Juventus to the title, and scored five goals as Juve reached the Champions League final! But Pavel was suspended for the final, and without him, Juve lost on penalties to Milan. But he was still named Best Midfielder at UEFA's 2003 Football Awards.

2004

CHELSEA CHASE!

After Roman Abramovich took over at Chelsea in the summer of 2003, Pavel Nedved was continually linked with a switch to The Blues. As one of Europe's top midfielders, it was obvious he was going to be linked with the West London club, and even the £25 million asking price didn't put Abramovich off. Nedved's agent Zdenek Nehoa said Chelsea had approached Juventus about the star and were keen to land him. But what made the story even more interesting was Chelsea wanted Sven Goran Eriksson to be their new manager, and Sven had already worked with Pavel at Lazio and enjoyed great success. The player himself kept quiet about Chelsea – only saying he had a contract in Italy until 2006 and wanted to honour it. Spoilsport!

2004

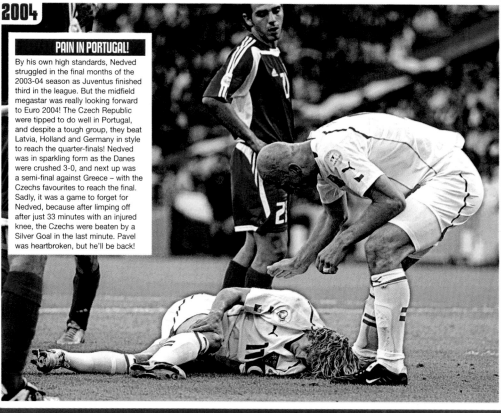

PAIN IN PORTUGAL!

By his own high standards, Nedved struggled in the final months of the 2003-04 season as Juventus finished third in the league. But the midfield megastar was really looking forward to Euro 2004! The Czech Republic were tipped to do well in Portugal, and despite a tough group, they beat Latvia, Holland and Germany in style to reach the quarter-finals! Nedved was in sparkling form as the Danes were crushed 3-0, and next up was a semi-final against Greece – with the Czechs favourites to reach the final. Sadly, it was a game to forget for Nedved, because after limping off after just 33 minutes with an injured knee, the Czechs were beaten by a Silver Goal in the last minute. Pavel was heartbroken, but he'll be back!

MATEJA KEZMAN · CHELSEA

WORLD SUPER STRIKERS

WSS

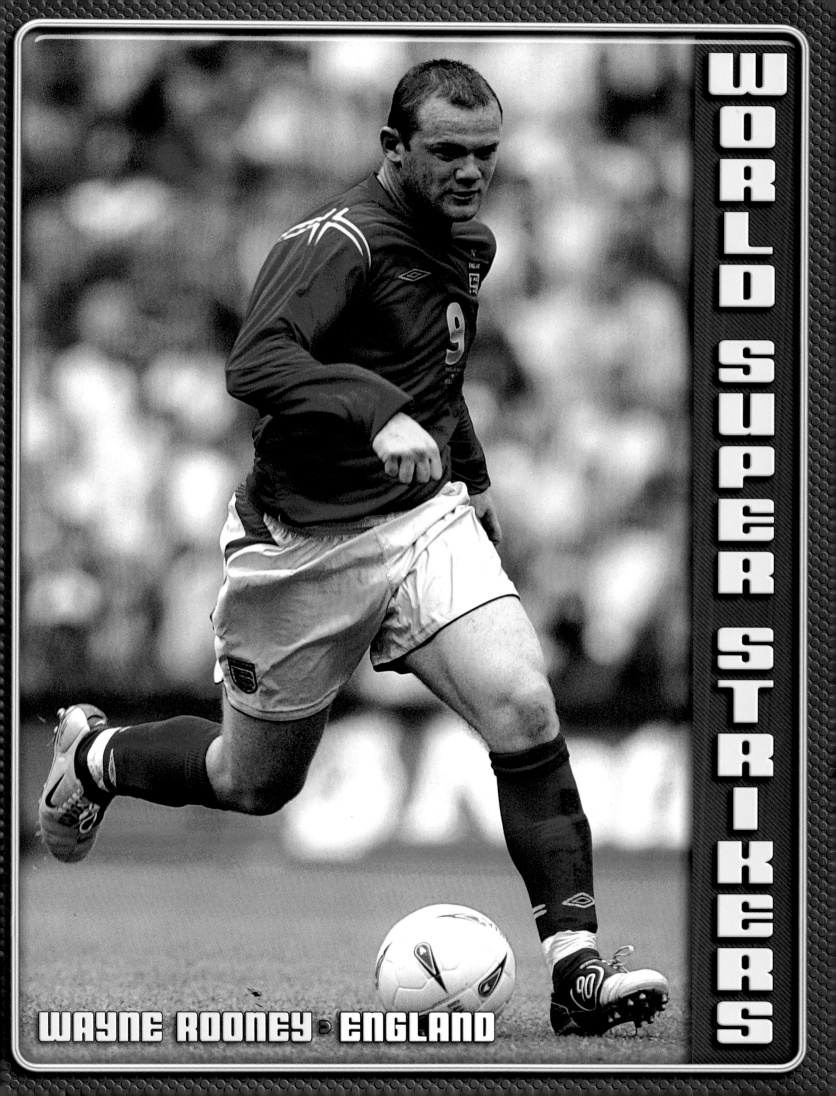

WORLD SUPER STRIKERS

WAYNE ROONEY · ENGLAND

50

TOP PREMIERSHIP PLAYERS OF 2003-04!

*Wanna know the real stars of last season's Premiership? Well, now you can check out the top 50 players – exclusively rated by **MATCHfacts!***

1

2

There were some outstanding individual performances in the Premiership last season. Thierry Henry was named the PFA's Player Of The Year, while Patrick Vieira and Sol Campbell both made massive contributions as Arsenal won the title.

Frank Lampard was the star of a new-look Chelsea side, Roy Keane proved the critics wrong by shining for Man. United, and Steven Gerrard was inspirational in helping Liverpool to a Champions League place.

Hitting the headlines for their goalscoring were Alan Shearer, Louis Saha, Mikael Forssell and Yakubu, while future England stars like Alan Smith, Shaun Wright-Phillips and Scott Parker all enjoyed excellent campaigns.

But which player topped our MATCHfacts ratings? Who performed week in, week out for their club? These are the most accurate ratings you'll find, because we watch every game of the season and we don't rate players by their reputation – they have to earn their mark out of ten every week! Now you can find out who's won our prestigious MATCHMAN Of The Year award, as we count down the 50 best players from last season…

PREVIOUS MATCHMAN OF THE YEAR WINNERS!

1997-1998	1998-1999	1999-2000	2000-2001	2001-2002	2002-2003
Dennis BERGKAMP	**Tony ADAMS**	**Paolo DI CANIO**	**Ryan GIGGS**	**Roy KEANE**	**Patrick VIEIRA**
Arsenal	*Arsenal*	*West Ham*	*Man. United*	*Man. United*	*Arsenal*

In MATCHfacts, everyone who plays more than 20 minutes in a game is awarded a rating out of ten, and the best player of the game is given a star rating. Players must have started at least 19 games in the 2003-04 season to be in the running for the MATCHMAN Of The Year award – the ultimate reward for excellence in every game!

PATRICK VIEIRA
Arsenal

Age: 28 ★ **Position:** Midfielder

Lowdown: Three players held the key to Arsenal winning the Premiership last season – Sol Campbell, Patrick Vieira and Thierry Henry. Big Sol was a rock in defence and Henry was in breathtaking form up front, but Vieira was the most consistent performer, and wins the MATCHMAN Of The Year award for the second season in a row! The Gunners didn't lose a single league game, because the opposition couldn't get past this huge man-mountain of a player! He proved to be the best in the world in his position – breaking down the opposition and launching lethal counter-attacks with powerful surges through the centre!

MATCHFACTS RATINGS

PLAYED	STARS	AVERAGE
29	8	7.31

> Why did Vieira finish with the best MATCHfacts rating?
For playing well in every single game! To be voted MATCHMAN Of The Year, you can't afford to have a bad match – you've got to get a good rating every time. Thierry Henry grabbed all the awards at the end of the season and he was fabulous to watch as usual, but MATCH went to every game and, on average, Vieira was the best player in the league!

> Why does he get such good ratings, then?
Just look at Vieira's contribution to the Arsenal team. He's almost impossible to beat in midfield with his huge frame and long legs, and when he goes forward he's almost impossible to tackle! The big man covers every blade of grass on the pitch, with 100 per cent effort for 90 minutes – tackling, heading, passing, roaring forward and scoring goals! The Gunners simply aren't the same team without their inspirational captain.

> What about his disciplinary record in the Premiership?
Paddy V didn't finish with a great record, and he lost his temper at Man. United last September – kicking Ruud van Nistelrooy and getting an instant red card. He got booked ten times, but he plays in the centre of midfield where tackling is a big part of his game, so what do you expect? If he suddenly changed his style, he wouldn't be the same player!

> What does the future hold for Vieira?
The French star has to pledge his future to Arsenal every year. But that's not surprising, because he's a world-class player, so other top clubs are always going to want him in their team. But Vieira seems happy with The Gunners, as long as the club is winning trophies and being successful. Don't rule out a move abroad in the future, though – Real Madrid are still desperate to bring him to Spain as their next 'Galactico'!

STEVEN GERRARD
Liverpool

Age: 24 ★ **Position:** Midfielder

Lowdown: Liverpool may have had a tough season, but without Steven Gerrard they wouldn't have got near their fourth-place Premiership finish. Stevie G's performances went up a level after taking over the captaincy from Sami Hyypia, as he grabbed games by the scruff of the neck and drove the team forward. He also matured with his new responsibility, picking up just three yellow cards in 34 games, and earned nine Star Ratings with his all-action displays to finish the season as one of the best midfielders in Europe. After Euro 2004, it looked like Gerrard was off to Chelsea for a staggering £30 million, but he chose to stay with The Reds and now hopes to win the title under new boss Rafael Benitez.

MATCHFACTS RATINGS

PLAYED	STARS	AVERAGE
34	9	7.26

THIERRY HENRY
Arsenal

Age: 27 ★ **Position:** Striker

Lowdown: It's a surprise to see Thierry Henry in third place here because he was the most exciting player to watch last season and the Premiership's leading scorer with 30 goals. Henry came close to stealing the award from Patrick Vieira with some awesome displays, combining ball control, pace and deadly finishing to scare the pants off defenders. His best moment was an individual effort in the crunch match against Liverpool, when he dribbled through the entire defence before slotting the ball into the corner of the net. But there were also brilliant free-kicks against Charlton and Blackburn, a 30-yard thunderbolt against Man. United, and four goals in one game against Leeds!

MATCHFACTS RATINGS

PLAYED	STARS	AVERAGE
37	10	7.19

4

FRANK LAMPARD
Chelsea

Age: 26 ★ **Position:** Midfielder

Lowdown: With Chelsea fielding a different team almost every week in 2003-04, Frank was the only Blues star to play in every league game. He was Chelsea's key man in midfield, despite the arrival of Claude Makelele and Scott Parker, and won 12 star ratings – the best total in this list. With his England career also rocketing after a fantastic Euro 2004 campaign, Lampard fully deserves to be fourth in this top 50 players shortlist.

MATCHFACTS RATINGS		
PLAYED	STARS	AVERAGE
38	12	7.08

5

ROY KEANE
Manchester United

Age: 33 ★ **Position:** Midfielder

Lowdown: Those who doubted Keano could still cut it at the highest level were left red-faced after a superb 2003-04 season. His highlight was three goals in four games in the autumn, including the winner at Leeds. With Keane's crunching tackles, work-rate and ear-bashing of his team-mates, he was once again United's top player.

MATCHFACTS RATINGS		
PLAYED	STARS	AVERAGE
28	6	7.00

6

JOHN TERRY
Chelsea

Age: 23 ★ **Position:** Defender

The highest-placed defender in the list, Terry pipped Gareth Southgate and Sami Hyypia with some top-class displays. The England man kept Marcel Desailly on the bench, and his powerful tackling only brought him five yellow cards from 33 matches. Terry often captained Chelsea and got the armband permanently in the summer.

MATCHFACTS RATINGS		
PLAYED	STARS	AVERAGE
33	5	6.94

7

GARETH SOUTHGATE
Middlesbrough

Age: 34 ★ **Position:** Defender

Lowdown: After lifting the Carling Cup – Middlesbrough's first ever trophy – 2003-04 was always going to be a memorable season for club captain Gareth Southgate. And had it not been for a nasty knee injury in April, he would have ended a brilliant campaign by boarding the plane to Portugal as part of England's Euro 2004 squad. But with six star ratings in 27 league games, he was still Boro's top player.

MATCHFACTS RATINGS		
PLAYED	STARS	AVERAGE
27	6	6.93

8

STEED MALBRANQUE
Fulham

Age: 24 ★ **Position:** Midfielder

Lowdown: The skilful winger was the key to Fulham's attack last season, linking midfield and attack with his jinking runs. Combining with Louis Saha, the pair carved open Premiership defences in the first half of the campaign. Malbranque was also unlucky not to make France's Euro 2004 squad, after scoring six league goals in 2003-04.

MATCHFACTS RATINGS		
PLAYED	STARS	AVERAGE
38	5	6.92

9

SAMI HYYPIA
Liverpool

Age: 30 ★ **Position:** Defender

Lowdown: The Finn struggled at the start of the season and lost the captain's armband to Steven Gerrard in October. With Stephane Henchoz injured, he had to form a partnership with Igor Biscan, who'd spent most of his career in midfield. But Hyypia rose to the challenge, regaining his top form to be a huge presence in defence.

MATCHFACTS RATINGS		
PLAYED	STARS	AVERAGE
38	5	6.89

10

ALAN SMITH
Leeds United

Age: 23 ★ **Position:** Striker

Lowdown: Although Smithy earned a top ten placing for his gutsy displays in 2003-04, it was a season to forget for him – Leeds were relegated and he had to leave his hometown club. In his preferred centre-forward role he scored nine goals for his struggling side – despite not netting at all in December and January – and at times his partnership with Mark Viduka was as good as ever. But when Leeds went down in May, Smith agreed a move to Man. United for £7 million and upset the Leeds fans badly in the process. But talent like his deserves to stay in the Premiership.

MATCHFACTS RATINGS		
PLAYED	STARS	AVERAGE
35	4	6.86

11

HENRI CAMARA
Wolves

Age: 27 ★ **Position:** Striker

Lowdown: Wolves splashed out £1.5 million on Henri Camara, hoping he could keep them in the Premiership. It didn't work, but the super-quick Senegal striker caught the eye with some exciting performances, and he bagged seven league goals in total – with six of those coming in his last nine appearances of the season.

MATCHFACTS RATINGS		
PLAYED	STARS	AVERAGE
30	5	6.80

12

MUZZY IZZET
Leicester City

Age: 29 ★ **Position:** Midfielder

Lowdown: Muzzy Izzet missed eight league games for Leicester in 2003-04 and they didn't win a single match without him – that's how important he was for The Foxes last season. The Turkey ace was a crucial link between midfield and attack, and although he only scored two league goals, he finished the season at the top of the Premiership goal assists chart. Moved to Birmingham City on a free transfer in the summer.

MATCHFACTS RATINGS		
PLAYED	STARS	AVERAGE
30	4	6.80

13

YOURI DJORKAEFF
Bolton Wanderers

Age: 36 ★ **Position:** Midfielder

Lowdown: The arrival of Kevin Davies at the beginning of the 2003-04 season helped to bring the best out of Djorkaeff. With someone to share the pressure of scoring goals, the Frenchman found more time and space to express himself, and he bagged eight league goals for Bolton – including a stunning scissor-kick against Charlton in April.

MATCHFACTS RATINGS		
PLAYED	STARS	AVERAGE
27	4	6.78

14

JAY-JAY OKOCHA
Bolton Wanderers

Age: 31 ★ **Position:** Midfielder

Lowdown: The Trotters trickster was once again a joy to watch in the Premiership with his breathtaking ability on the ball. Although he didn't score a league goal in 2003-04, he scored some real crackers on the way to the Carling Cup final and deservedly made the shortlist for the PFA Players' Player Of The Year award.

MATCHFACTS RATINGS		
PLAYED	STARS	AVERAGE
35	5	6.77

15

SCOTT PARKER
Chelsea

Age: 23 ★ **Position:** Midfielder

Lowdown: After 12 years at Charlton, Parker decided last season it was time to move on and further his career. A great first half of the 2003-04 term for The Addicks – where he bossed the midfield, scored a cracking double at Southampton and made his England debut – alerted Chelsea, and The Blues splashed out £10 million for him in January. At Stamford Bridge, he had to get used to a rotation policy and playing on the wing, but he clearly enjoyed the step up. The challenge now is to be just as consistent for Chelsea as he was for Charlton.

MATCHFACTS RATINGS		
PLAYED	STARS	AVERAGE
31	4	6.77

16

OLOF MELLBERG
Aston Villa

Age: 27 ★ **Position:** Defender

Lowdown: Olof was actually dropped for Villa's first league game of the 2003-04 season, but the skipper bounced back to become one of the team's most important players. The centre-back was solid throughout as The Villans finished sixth in the Premiership, and chipped in with a goal in the 4-0 drubbing of Midlands rivals Wolves!

MATCHFACTS RATINGS		
PLAYED	STARS	AVERAGE
33	4	6.76

17

LOUIS SAHA
Manchester United

Age: 26 ★ **Position:** Striker

Lowdown: Saha roared into action at the start of 2003-04 with 13 goals in 21 games for Fulham, and it was that form which got him a £12.82 million move to Old Trafford. Despite some niggling injuries, he still netted a promising seven goals in 12 appearances for The Red Devils, including a debut strike against Southampton.

MATCHFACTS RATINGS		
PLAYED	STARS	AVERAGE
33	3	6.76

18

JUNINHO
Middlesbrough

Age: 31 ★ **Position:** Midfielder

Lowdown: The little Brazilian is knocking on now – not that you could tell by his displays in 2003-04. On top of the usual tricks we've come to expect, the samba star also weighed in with eight Premiership goals, which included a brace against Blackburn and another double as Boro beat Man. United 3-2 in their own backyard!

MATCHFACTS RATINGS		
PLAYED	STARS	AVERAGE
31	5	6.76

19

ROBERT PIRES
Arsenal

Age: 30 ★ **Position:** Midfielder

Lowdown: Robert Pires was effectively Thierry Henry's strike partner last season, bagging 14 Premiership goals and setting up a truckload for his team-mates. The France international hadn't changed positions, though – he played all season as a left winger, but he used his magical skills and burst of pace to support the Gunners frontline. One of the highlights of his season came against Liverpool, when he curled a 25-yard winner to keep Arsenal a point clear at the top of the Premiership.

MATCHFACTS RATINGS		
PLAYED	STARS	AVERAGE
36	4	6.75

20

ARJAN DE ZEEUW
Portsmouth

Age: 34 ★ **Position:** Defender

Lowdown: When the Dutchman last played in the Premiership with Barnsley six years ago, he struggled and the Tykes were relegated. But with Pompey in 2003-04, he proved he'd stepped up, putting in the kind of rock-solid displays that earned the South Coast club a surprise 1-0 win against Man. United at Fratton Park.

MATCHFACTS RATINGS		
PLAYED	STARS	AVERAGE
36	3	6.75

21

GAIZKA MENDIETA
Middlesbrough

Age: 30 ★ **Position:** Midfielder

Lowdown: As a former UEFA Midfielder Of The Year and a man who cost Lazio £28 million in 2001, Gaizka Mendieta went to Boro with a big reputation – and it didn't take long for the artful midfielder to show the Boro fans exactly why! Mendi, who originally joined Boro on loan from Lazio in the summer of 2003, brought real class to the side despite a quiet spell after Christmas – and scored in the 5-3 win over Birmingham.

MATCHFACTS RATINGS		
PLAYED	STARS	AVERAGE
31	0	6.75

22

RICHARD DUNNE
Manchester City

Age: 24 ★ **Position:** Defender

Lowdown: After being criticised for under-performing in the early part of his Manchester City career, Dunne showed why the club paid £3 million for him in 2000. The Irishman was a regular at centre-back with Sylvain Distin by the end of the season, proving a strong match for any Premiership forward he came up against.

MATCHFACTS RATINGS		
PLAYED	STARS	AVERAGE
29	3	6.72

23

JOSEPH YOBO
Everton

Age: 24 ★ **Position:** Defender

Lowdown: Yobo was one of the highlights in a poor campaign for Everton. The Nigerian ace was strong and quick, but the team missed him when he left to play in the African Nations Cup. He bagged his first goal for Everton against Newcastle in April though, and won the club's Young Player Of The Year award at the end of the season!

MATCHFACTS RATINGS		
PLAYED	STARS	AVERAGE
28	3	6.71

24

ANDY O'BRIEN
Newcastle United

Age: 25 ★ **Position:** Defender

Lowdown: O'Brien shone in a Newcastle defence that got a lot of unfair criticism in 2003-04. The 25-year-old formed a solid partnership with Jonathan Woodgate, often taking more responsibility when Woodgate was injured. O'Brien didn't pick up any star ratings, but his 6.71 average showed he was Newcastle's Mr Consistency!

MATCHFACTS RATINGS		
PLAYED	STARS	AVERAGE
28	0	6.71

25

DAVID DUNN
Birmingham City

Age: 24 ★ **Position:** Midfielder

Lowdown: Dunn's Birmingham career got off to a real flyer in 2003-04 after his £5.5 million transfer from Blackburn. The tricky midfielder scored the winner against Spurs on his debut and again at Newcastle two games later, and won rave reviews playing on the right wing or behind the striker. But a hamstring injury ruined the second half of his season and he barely kicked a ball for three months. Birmingham badly missed his skill and energy.

MATCHFACTS RATINGS		
PLAYED	STARS	AVERAGE
21	1	6.71

26

EDWIN VAN DER SAR
Fulham

Age: 33 ★ **Position:** Goalkeeper

Lowdown: Edwin van der Sar's consistency helped keep Fulham in the UEFA Cup shake-up for most of the 2003-04 season. The big Dutchman was solid in all departments, but shone in one-on-one situations where he repeatedly saved the game for his team. He also made brilliant penalty saves against Middlesbrough and Liverpool.

MATCHFACTS RATINGS		
PLAYED	STARS	AVERAGE
37	2	6.70

27

KOLO TOURE
Arsenal

Age: 23 ★ **Position:** Defender

Lowdown: In desperate need of a solid partner for Sol Campbell, Arsenal turned to Kolo Toure. The Ivory Coast colossus slotted in brilliantly at centre-back, and despite his lack of experience, he was strong, commanding in the air and quick on the turn. He improved as the season went on, keeping big-name strikers quiet and earning rave reviews. At the end of 2003-04 he was shortlisted for the PFA Young Player Of The Year award.

MATCHFACTS RATINGS		
PLAYED	STARS	AVERAGE
37	1	6.68

28

NICKY HUNT
Bolton Wanderers

Age: 21 ★ **Position:** Defender

Lowdown: Nicky began his first full season as a Bolton regular with a visit to Old Trafford on the opening day of the 2003-04 season. The Trotters lost 4-0, but fortunately Sam Allardyce kept faith with the youngster and he went on to become one of the stars of Bolton's season, even scoring his first goal for the club against Liverpool!

MATCHFACTS RATINGS		
PLAYED	STARS	AVERAGE
31	1	6.68

29

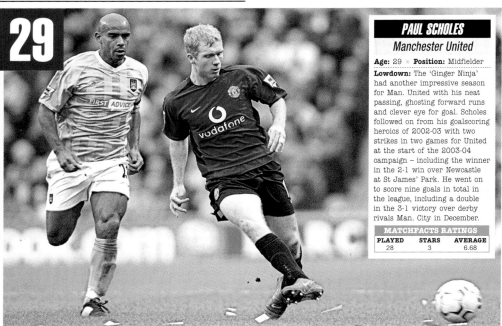

PAUL SCHOLES
Manchester United

Age: 29 ★ **Position:** Midfielder

Lowdown: The 'Ginger Ninja' had another impressive season for Man. United with his neat passing, ghosting forward runs and clever eye for goal. Scholes followed on from his goalscoring heroics of 2002-03 with two strikes in two games for United at the start of the 2003-04 campaign – including the winner in the 2-1 win over Newcastle at St James' Park. He went on to score nine goals in total in the league, including a double in the 3-1 victory over derby rivals Man. City in December.

MATCHFACTS RATINGS		
PLAYED	STARS	AVERAGE
28	3	6.68

30

JAMIE CARRAGHER
Liverpool

Age: 26 ★ **Position:** Defender

Lowdown: It was a season of two halves for Carragher, who only played five games before breaking his leg in September 2003. The versatile Liverpool defender returned four months later, playing first at right-back and then at centre-back. His excellent form impressed Sven Goran Eriksson, who included him in his Euro 2004 squad.

MATCHFACTS RATINGS		
PLAYED	STARS	AVERAGE
22	0	6.68

31

KENNY CUNNINGHAM
Birmingham City

Age: 33 ★ **Position:** Defender

Lowdown: The Birmingham ace was as solid as ever, as Steve Bruce's side chased a European spot until the final weeks of the season. The skipper played 36 games – more than any of his team-mates – and helped the club keep 15 clean sheets in the league. The 33-year-old said it was a challenge staying in the team with Matt Upson and Martin Taylor snapping at his heels, but he can be proud of yet another good campaign.

MATCHFACTS RATINGS		
PLAYED	STARS	AVERAGE
36	2	6.67

32

ALEX RAE
Wolves

Age: 34 ★ **Position:** Midfielder

Lowdown: The fiery midfielder always gave 100 per cent for Wolves, despite their relegation. Rae's battling qualities got him in trouble with refs – he was booked ten times and sent off against Middlesbrough – but he scored five Premiership goals, including a long-range cracker at Bolton. Moved to Rangers in the summer of 2004.

MATCHFACTS RATINGS		
PLAYED	STARS	AVERAGE
33	4	6.67

33

SHAUN WRIGHT-PHILLIPS
Manchester City

Age: 24 ★ **Position:** Midfielder

Lowdown: Although Shaun has been at City since 1998, it was not until the 2003-04 season that he caught the eye with some top displays. Arguably City's best player, he bagged seven league goals, including a stunner against United at the City Of Manchester Stadium, and was rewarded with a call-up to the England squad.

MATCHFACTS RATINGS		
PLAYED	STARS	AVERAGE
34	2	6.65

34

NIGEL MARTYN
Everton

Age: 38 ★ **Position:** Goalkeeper

Lowdown: The veteran stopper had signed from Leeds United as back-up for Richard Wright on the September 1 transfer deadline, but he ended up as Everton's first-choice 'keeper for most of the 2003-04 season. Following an injury to Wright, Martyn kept ten clean sheets and was deservedly voted the club's Player Of The Season.

MATCHFACTS RATINGS		
PLAYED	STARS	AVERAGE
34	1	6.65

35

RIO FERDINAND
Manchester United

Age: 25 ★ **Position:** Defender

Lowdown: Rio missed a chunk of the 2003-04 season through suspension after missing a drugs test in September, but he was in fine form during the first five months of the campaign. The Red Devils only conceded 14 goals from the 20 games he played in, and critics said United's title challenge fell away when Rio was missing.

MATCHFACTS RATINGS		
PLAYED	STARS	AVERAGE
20	0	6.65

36

MARK SCHWARZER
Middlesbrough

Age: 31 ★ **Position:** Goalkeeper

Lowdown: Dependable Aussie 'keeper Mark Schwarzer was as consistent as ever for Boro last season, and he played in all but two of his side's Premiership games. His fantastic form also carried into the Carling Cup, where he saved a penalty in the quarter-final shoot-out with Spurs and played brilliantly against Arsenal in the semis.

MATCHFACTS RATINGS		
PLAYED	STARS	AVERAGE
36	1	6.64

37

RYAN GIGGS
Manchester United

Age: 30 ★ **Position:** Midfielder

Lowdown: The Welsh wizard turned 30 in November 2003, but with an injury-free season he again terrorised defenders with his skill and pace. Giggsy netted two goals on the opening day against Bolton – including a free-kick – but possibly his best moment was his double in United's 2-1 win over Liverpool at Anfield in November. The No.11 netted seven Premiership goals in total and provided some crucial assists along the way.

MATCHFACTS RATINGS		
PLAYED	STARS	AVERAGE
33	4	6.64

38

SYLVAIN DISTIN
Manchester City

Age: 26 ★ **Position:** Defender

Lowdown: As an ever-present for Man. City last season, Distin played a huge part in keeping his side in the Premiership. City didn't exactly have a solid back four, conceding 54 goals in total, but Sylvain at least deserves some credit. Named captain of the side in pre-season by Kevin Keegan, he repaid his manager's faith with a series of athletic displays at the heart of City's defence. Won more star ratings than any of his team-mates.

MATCHFACTS RATINGS		
PLAYED	STARS	AVERAGE
38	4	6.63

39

JLLOYD SAMUEL
Aston Villa

Age: 23 ★ **Position:** Defender

Lowdown: Samuel made great strides during his first season under David O'Leary. Always impressive going forward, the left-back also worked on his defensive skills, playing every minute of every league game and scoring two goals – both against Charlton. JLloyd also earned a well deserved call-up to the England squad.

MATCHFACTS RATINGS		
PLAYED	STARS	AVERAGE
38	2	6.63

40

SOL CAMPBELL
Arsenal

Age: 29 ★ **Position:** Defender

Lowdown: Campbell was one of the main reasons why Arsenal went 38 league games without losing, conceding just 26 goals. After getting sent-off against Everton in September, he led by example in defence with his strong tackling, heading and inspirational leadership to claim his second Premiership title with The Gunners.

MATCHFACTS RATINGS		
PLAYED	STARS	AVERAGE
35	1	6.63

41

MATT UPSON
Birmingham City

Age: 25 ★ **Position:** Defender

Lowdown: Upson could have rivalled Kenny Cunningham as Birmingham's top defender if he hadn't suffered an ankle injury in January. But he still collected two star ratings from his 30 Premiership games.

MATCHFACTS RATINGS		
PLAYED	STARS	AVERAGE
30	2	6.63

42

ALAN STUBBS
Everton

Age: 32 ★ **Position:** Defender

Lowdown: Stubbsy's experience, strength and leadership skills helped steer The Toffees through their fight against relegation in 2003-04. The former Bolton and Celtic centre-back – who was actually released by Everton as a teenager before returning to the club in 2001 – showed the passion, grit and determination of a terrace fan to drag his side to safety. The Toffees kept eight clean sheets with Stubbs in the line-up, and his influence on others was key to survival.

MATCHFACTS RATINGS		
PLAYED	STARS	AVERAGE
27	0	6.63

43

ALAN SHEARER
Newcastle United

Age: 33 ★ **Position:** Striker

Lowdown: He isn't getting any younger, but last season Alan Shearer showed he still knows where the goal is. The veteran Newcastle striker hit 22 goals in 37 games and picked up four star ratings along the way.

MATCHFACTS RATINGS		
PLAYED	STARS	AVERAGE
37	4	6.62

44

MIKAEL FORSSELL
Birmingham City

Age: 23 ★ **Position:** Striker

Lowdown: It was a smart piece of business when Birmingham took Mikael Forssell on loan from Chelsea for the 2003-04 campaign. The talented Finland striker was desperate to play every week and finished his first full Premiership season with an impressive 17 goals from 32 games. Quick, strong and with tricks up his sleeve, Forssell showed Chelsea what they were missing in front of goal. Surprisingly, he has been allowed to stay with The Blues for another season.

MATCHFACTS RATINGS		
PLAYED	STARS	AVERAGE
32	3	6.62

45

PAUL INCE
Wolves

Age: 36 ★ **Position:** Midfielder

Lowdown: Paul Ince delayed retirement for another crack at top-flight footy and was an influential figure for Wolves. His experience and class didn't stop relegation, but the former England man was consistent throughout. Some of his tackles were a bit wild, though – he was booked 14 times and sent off on the last day of the season!

MATCHFACTS RATINGS		
PLAYED	STARS	AVERAGE
32	0	6.62

46

GARY SPEED
Newcastle United

Age: 35 ★ **Position:** Midfielder

Lowdown: Another golden oldie, Gary Speed showed in 2003-04 that he was just as fit and still as good as team-mates almost half his age! The Wales star brought brains and experience to a young Newcastle midfield, and with three star ratings he showed the youngsters the way forward. Joined Bolton for a fee of £750,000 in the summer.

MATCHFACTS RATINGS		
PLAYED	STARS	AVERAGE
38	3	6.61

47

JUSSI JAASKELAINEN
Bolton Wanderers

Age: 29 ★ **Position:** Goalkeeper

Lowdown: Jussi played every Premiership game for Bolton in 2003-04, and his consistency between the sticks helped keep Bolton well away from the relegation zone and finish in a highly respectable eighth place!

MATCHFACTS RATINGS		
PLAYED	STARS	AVERAGE
38	0	6.61

48

PAUL DICKOV
Leicester City

Age: 32 ★ **Position:** Striker

Lowdown: Dickov's nickname is 'The Wasp', because he buzzes around everywhere and is a real nuisance! The striker hit 11 goals, and even though The Foxes were relegated, Dickov earned a move to Blackburn.

MATCHFACTS RATINGS		
PLAYED	STARS	AVERAGE
35	3	6.60

49

LEE CLARK
Fulham

Age: 31 ★ **Position:** Midfielder

Lowdown: Clark put a poor two years under Jean Tigana well behind him in 2003-04 as he established himself as Fulham's midfield lynchpin. Under new boss Chris Coleman he was back to his best, snapping and snarling in midfield. Crucially, he was injured for the last 11 games of the season as the club fell short of making Europe.

MATCHFACTS RATINGS		
PLAYED	STARS	AVERAGE
25	2	6.60

50

DIETMAR HAMANN
Liverpool

Age: 30 ★ **Position:** Midfielder

Lowdown: Steven Gerrard may have been Liverpool's driving force in midfield, but Dietmar Hamann did his usual excellent job of breaking down attacks and nicking the ball away from the opposition. He missed the first four months of the season with a nasty shin injury, but The Reds improved when he came back into the team, with his highlight being a sensational 25-yard volley in a 3-0 victory over Portsmouth in March.

MATCHFACTS RATINGS		
PLAYED	STARS	AVERAGE
25	0	6.60

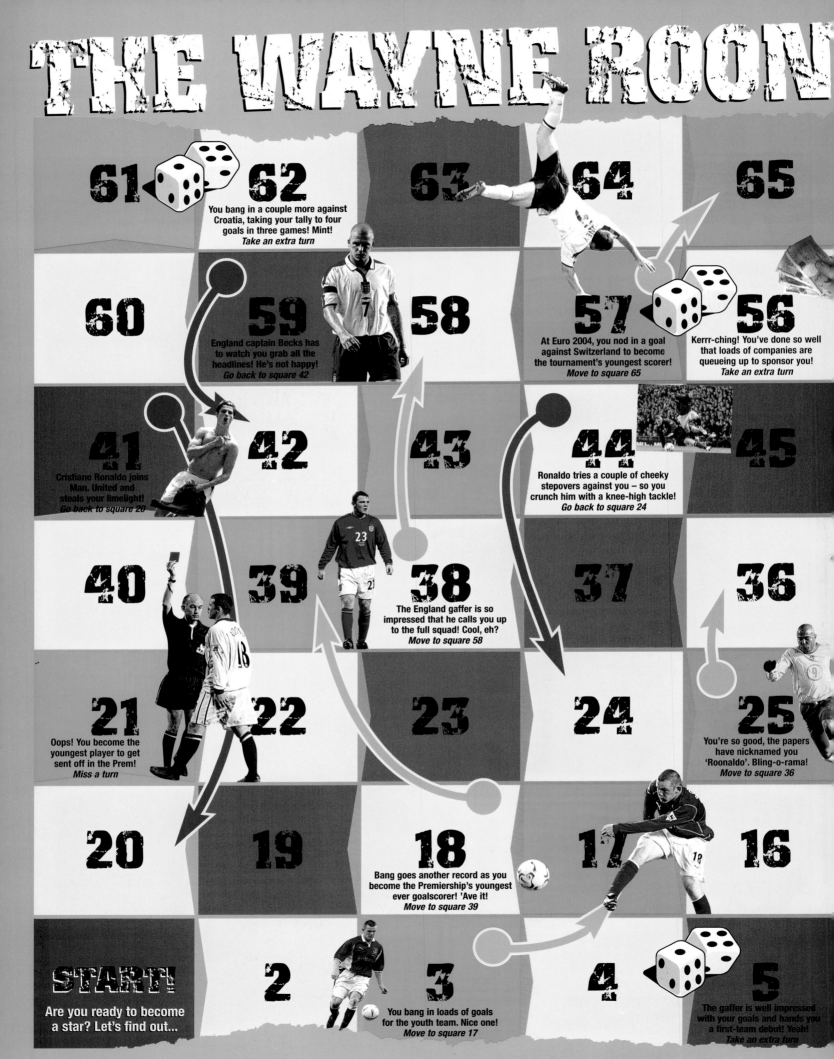

61

62
You bang in a couple more against Croatia, taking your tally to four goals in three games! Mint!
Take an extra turn

63

64

65

60

59
England captain Becks has to watch you grab all the headlines! He's not happy!
Go back to square 42

58

57
At Euro 2004, you nod in a goal against Switzerland to become the tournament's youngest scorer!
Move to square 65

56
Kerrr-ching! You've done so well that loads of companies are queueing up to sponsor you!
Take an extra turn

41
Cristiano Ronaldo joins Man. United and steals your limelight!
Go back to square 20

42

43

44
Ronaldo tries a couple of cheeky stepovers against you – so you crunch him with a knee-high tackle!
Go back to square 24

45

40

39

38
The England gaffer is so impressed that he calls you up to the full squad! Cool, eh?
Move to square 58

37

36

21
Oops! You become the youngest player to get sent off in the Prem!
Miss a turn

22

23

24

25
You're so good, the papers have nicknamed you 'Roonaldo'. Bling-o-rama!
Move to square 36

20

19

18
Bang goes another record as you become the Premiership's youngest ever goalscorer! 'Ave it!
Move to square 39

17

16

START!
Are you ready to become a star? Let's find out...

2

3
You bang in loads of goals for the youth team. Nice one!
Move to square 17

4

5
The gaffer is well impressed with your goals and hands you a first-team debut! Yeah!
Take an extra turn

MATCHMAN'S QUIZ

YO, YO, YO, QUIZ DUDES AND DUDETTES! HERE'S WHERE WE FIND OUT IF YER A TITLE CHASIN' FOOTY GENIUS, OR A FOOTY DUFUS DOOMED FOR RELEGATION! CHECK OFF YER ANSWERS FROM ME FIVE SUPER TUFF QUIZZES THAT YA DID EARLIER IN ME ANNUAL. THEN ADD UP YER POINTS TOTAL OUT OF 250 BEFORE SEEIN' HOW YOU'VE DONE! GOOD LUCK!

201-250
YOU'RE MAN OF THE MATCH!
What a performance! If you've topped da 200 mark, you've just become a fully qualified member of me MATCH Massive – so big-up to ya, dude or dudette! You is in da Premier League of footy brainboxes!

151-200
YOU'VE BAGGED A HAT-TRICK!
Wickedy-wicked! A big shout goes out to ya for yer tip-top score – respec'! Ya ain't quite made it to da top yet, but wiv a bit more footy homework, it ain't gonna be long before yer da star of da whole show!

101-150
YOU'RE A STEADY-EDDIE!
Nice one! I recks you're an up-and-coming youngster when it comes to footy knowledge. There's still a bit of work for ya to do, but you is defo on da right track – I ain't worried about ya! Keep up da good work!

51-100
YOU'VE BEEN BOOKED!
That's a caution! I 'as got me book out and given ya a yellow card for dis dodgy showin'! If you're gonna make it in dis game, you've gotta watch loads more footy – and make sure ya read MATCH every single week!

Under 51
YOU'VE SCORED AN OWN GOAL!
Uh-oh! Is you havin' a laugh wiv dis score? Do ya ever read MATCH? I reckon you is either a cricket fan wot 'as picked up me footy annual by accident – or ya just guessed yer way thru me quizzes! No, no no!

QUIZ 1 page 26!
HELP PERCY!
1. Ledley King
2. Robert Pires
3. Fernando Torres
4. Antonio Cassano
5. Alexei Smertin

Smertin.

RONALDINHO QUIZ!
1. £21 million
2. PSG
3. Ten
4. David Seaman
5. R

Ronaldinho.

CHANGIN' SHIRTS!
Wilfred Bouma
Olof Mellberg

WORD SEARCH!

DREAM TEAM!
RB: Paulo Ferreira
CB: Igor Stepanovs
CB: Traianos Dellas
LB: Gianluca Zambrotta
RM: Stelios Giannakopoulos
CM: Zinedine Zidane
CM: Edgar Davids
LM: Pavel Nedved
S: Zlatan Ibrahimovic
S: Kevin Kuranyi

QUIZ 2 page 40!
PERCY'S TWUE OR FALSE!
1. False
2. True
3. True
4. False
5. False

Seedorf.

TRANSFER TRACKER!
1997 - 2000 Real Madrid
2000 - 2002 Inter Milan

SPOT THE DIFFERENCE!
Beckham wearing No.9
Star on Becks's shirt
Rooney's Umbro badge
Rooney's blue shorts
Scholes's Fairplay logo

WHO AM I?
Francesco Totti

ANSWERS!

ULTIMATE CHALLENGE!

1. Rafael Benitez
2. Helder Postiga
3. Arsenal
4. Inter Milan
5. Kevin Keegan
6. Pinhead
7. Denmark
8. Crystal Palace
9. Emile Heskey
10. Norwich

Heskey.

CHAMPO LEAGUE CHALLENGE!

Raul
Hargreaves
Stam
Maldini
Deco

NATIONAL DRESS!

Darren Fletcher

Fletcher.

KIT MATCH-UP!

1. D
2. A
3. B
4. E
5. C

SPOT THE DIFFERENCE!

No.21 on shorts
Charisteas's shorts logo
Charisteas's boot is red
Dellas wearing No.6
Stripe on Dellas's sock

Albelda.

CAP IN HAND!

b) 63

PASTA OR PAELLA?

Cassano - PASTA
Luque - PAELLA
Albelda - PAELLA
Pirlo - PASTA
Oddo - PASTA

Cassano.

DREAM TEAM!

GK: Robert Green
CB: Zat Knight
CB: Mark Fish
LB: Gary Naysmith
RM: Freddie Ljungberg
CM: Eric Djemba-Djemba
CM: Muzzy Izzet
LM: Harry Kewell
S: James Beattie
S: Craig Bellamy

SPORTS MAD!

Milan Baros

Baros.

TROPHY TRACKER!

2001 - Bayern Munich
2002 - Real Madrid

Real Madrid.
...IONS
...e Final - Glasgow 2002

QUIZ 3 page 50!

ENGLAND QUIZ!

1. Switzerland
2. David Beckham
3. 2001
4. Umbro
5. Brazil
6. None
7. Sir Alf Ramsey
8. Canada
9. Macedonia
10. Six

ANDRIY SHEVCHENKO QUIZ!

1. Ukraine
2. Dynamo Kiev
3. £16 million
4. Seven
5. 2003

QUIZ 4 page 60!

HEAD SPIN!

Kevin Kuranyi

Kuranyi.

BARCELONA QUIZ!

1. Nou Camp
2. One
3. Second
4. Frank Rijkaard
5. True

QUIZ 5 page 72!

SPOT THE SPIES!

Iain Dowie
David Moyes
Chris Coleman
Jose Mourinho
Alex Ferguson

WHAT'S YOUR JOB?

1. D
2. E
3. A
4. B
5. C

FINAL WHISTLE!

SEE YA LATER!

NICE ONE, MATCH READERS! YOU READ THE LOT!

A BIG ROUND OF APPLAUSE FOR THE MATCH READERS, LADS!

YOU GUYS ARE THE REAL FOOTY FANS!

2005 HERE WE COME!

Look out for these top ten things next year!

Dave Becks and England marching through the 2006 World Cup qualifiers!

Ferguson, Wenger and Mourinho all battling it out for the top trophies!

Another really expensive summer signing at moneybags Real Madrid!

The last FA Cup final to be held at Cardiff's ace Millennium Stadium!

Young guns like Jermain Defoe and Chris Kirkland making the England team!

The 50th European Cup final at the Ataturk Olympic Stadium!

Thierry Henry and Ruud van Nistelrooy battling it out for the Golden Boot again!

The wicked new Wembley stadium – complete with huge arch – taking shape!

Wayne Rooney kicking international defenders' butts for England!

Exclusive interviews, quizzes and top prizes in MATCH every single week!

①

THE PREMIERSHIP IS THIS WAY, SKILLS FANS!

THE ENGLISH LEAGUE RULES, FOR SURE!

GET IN! I'M IN THE BEST LEAGUE IN THE WORLD, AT LAST!

Henry, Van Nistelrooy, Baros, Kezman, Shearer, Okocha, Anelka and the rest of MATCH's top footy mates reckon the Premiership rocks - and we reckon wicked superstars like that are never wrong! Get in!

10 REASONS WHY...

THE PREMIERSHIP IS THE BEST LEAGUE IN THE WORLD!

②  The players in Italy's Serie A are technically pretty good, but the matches are boring and you won't see the amazing attacking goal-fests you get in the Premiership!

③  Germany's Bundesliga is skint, but thanks to Roman's Chelski Empire and Moneybags Man. United, the Premiership can afford the best players around!

④  Le Championnat in France doesn't always attract many fans, but our Premiership grounds are packed with thousands of loony supporters every single week!

⑤  There are some pants stadiums in Holland's Ere Divisie, but with Old Trafford, Anfield, St James' Park and The City Of Manchester Stadium, our footy homes rule!

⑥  Rangers and Celtic kick everyone's butts in the Scottish Premier League, but in the Premiership the smaller teams often shock the footy giants!

⑦  Spain's Primera Liga has some top teams like Real Madrid, Barcelona and Valencia, but their fans are too fickle and boo their team if they start losing!

⑧  The Portuguese Campeonato Nacional is pretty good, but the mop-haired stars spend all the time rolling around on the floor and conning the referee! Boo!

⑨  Until the players in the American MLS start calling it 'footy' instead of 'soccer', they'll still be a bunch of hamburger-munching Yankee losers!

⑩  The Brazilian championship is filled with loads of flash tricksters - so it's a shame they always end up scrapping with each other on the pitch! Oof!

They think it's all over – but it ain't!

The referee's about to blow the final whistle on your 2005 MATCH Annual, but not even the geezer in black can stop you picking up a wicked copy of MATCH every single week! MATCH is the biggest-selling weekly footy magazine in the country and it's packed with loads of cool interviews, stories, games and competitions – so make sure you bag a copy every Tuesday!